Praise for *Mentor*

Mentoring matters, and we need to get it right. The guidance ı.. ı ied and thoroughly informative book will undoubtedly help, as Haili Hughes gu.₋ ₋s as to how effective mentoring from expert colleagues can provide our new and novice teachers with the platform to thrive, succeed and grow.

Chris Moyse, Head of Staff Development, Bridgwater and Taunton College Trust

This is a superb resource for mentors at a time when the role has finally been given the recognition it deserves and is therefore more important than ever. Haili combines a deeply reflective, evidence based approach with a fantastically practical and well-organised format. This makes *Mentoring in Schools* a book that lends itself both to a long, thought-provoking read and to the possibility of being dipped into at point of need.

Professor Samantha Twiselton, OBE, Senior Academic and Chair of the DfE Advisory Group for the ITT Core Content Framework

Like all great books, *Mentoring in Schools* will have impact beyond the intended audience. It is an excellent text not just for mentors but as a useful aide-memoire for our own knowledge, understanding and practice of the principles behind the Early Career Framework. Its compelling blend of research, excellent summaries and insights from focus groups will make this a standard text across the sector.

Mary Myatt, author of *Back on Track* and curator of The Soak

Mentoring in Schools is the book that so many schools and mentors have been crying out for: a comprehensive, no-nonsense guide to mentoring which should serve to both enhance the effectiveness and raise the profile of mentors in our schools, while simultaneously providing a rich and beautifully curated collation of research and resources to support them in their role. Haili's detailed analysis of best practice along-side existing published research is combined to form an easy-to-navigate, deftly articulated and essential guide to the role of mentor. A long overdue handbook for those carrying out this vital work in supporting our early career colleagues.

Emma Turner, Research and CPD Lead, Discovery Schools Trust, and founder of #NewEd

In *Mentoring in Schools*, Haili Hughes exemplifies the ways in which effective mentoring can ensure that new and trainee teachers have an exciting and empowering start to their teaching roles, providing them with the tools to sustain a fulfilling career in education. Drawing on her experience in academia, Hughes combines the voices of new teachers through qualitative interviews, with a systematic approach to the new Early Career Framework, illustrating what effective mentoring looks like on both a cultural and practical level.

Packed with precise and clearly explained pedagogical theory, this book is a great text for managing mentors, ITT providers and teaching and learning leads to get their teeth into when considering the efficacy of both their beginner teacher provision and their in-house mentor training. To argue the tantamount importance of the mentoring role, and for anyone keen to take this role seriously, *Mentoring in Schools* is a vital companion to refer back to again and again.

Emma Sheppard, founder of The MTPT Project

Mentoring in Schools provides a succinct exploration of what is required to be a successful mentor in a school. Haili guides readers through the Teachers' Standards, offering the prospective or established mentor a wealth of strategies and interventions with which to support their mentee. Utilising her own original collection of relevant case studies, as well as her own extensive experience, Haili offers excellent advice and guidance to anyone charged with mentoring the next generation of teachers. Above all, Haili is an excellent writer and her passion for the profession clearly translates into the pages of this book. I highly recommend this book to anyone embarking on that special journey of supporting a teacher colleague.

Tom Rogers, history teacher, blogger, and director of TeachMeetIcons and Edudate

Haili's book provides mentors with a handy step-by-step guide through the Early Career Framework, enabling them to provide support and instruction to their mentees. It provides a wealth of research, explanation, examples, practical advice and activities to underpin some of the most effective approaches in ensuring high expectations for all and improving teaching.

Mentoring in Schools will prove invaluable to all mentors, whether they are experienced in or new to the role, providing a clear guide to those working with early career teachers and indeed anyone who could benefit from some mentoring regardless of stage. It is certainly a book I would recommend to all who want to reflect on their practice as a mentor.

Zoe Enser, Lead English Adviser, The Education People, and author and blogger

Haili Hughes

Mentoring in Schools

How to become an expert colleague

Forewords by Professor Rachel Lofthouse and Reuben Moore

Crown House Publishing Limited
www.crownhouse.co.uk

First published by
Crown House Publishing Limited
Crown Buildings, Bancyfelin, Carmarthen, Wales, SA33 5ND, UK
www.crownhouse.co.uk

and

Crown House Publishing Company LLC
PO Box 2223, Williston, VT 05495, USA
www.crownhousepublishing.com

© Haili Hughes, 2021

The right of Haili Hughes to be identified as the author of this work has been asserted by her in accordance with the Copyright, Designs and Patents Act 1988.

First published 2021. Reprinted 2021.

Cover image © Bro Vector – stock.adobe.com.
Pages 36 and 52, ladder images © Oleksandr Rozhkov – stock.adobe.com.

Quotes from Ofsted and Department for Education documents used in this publication have been approved under an Open Government Licence. Please see http://www.nationalarchives.gov.uk/doc/open-government-licence/version/3.

Page 31, photograph © Corrie Halford, used with kind permission. Page 32, photographs © Fe Brewer, used with kind permission. Pages 82 and 83, photographs © Lisa Marie Ford, used with kind permission. Pages 86–87, Figure 4.2 © Gary Hammond, from 'Cognitive load theory in the English classroom'. *The Deep Bare Garden* (29 November 2018). Available at: https://thedeepbaregarden.wordpress.com/2018/11/29/cognitive-load-theory-in-the-english-classroom. Used with kind permission.

Crown House Publishing has no responsibility for the persistence or accuracy of URLs for external or third-party websites referred to in this publication, and does not guarantee that any content on such websites is, or will remain, accurate or appropriate.

British Library Cataloguing-in-Publication Data

A catalogue entry for this book is available from the British Library.

Print ISBN 978-178583523-0
Mobi ISBN 978-178583544-5
ePub ISBN 978-178583545-2
ePDF ISBN 978-178583546-9

LCCN 2020952158

Printed and bound in the UK by
Charlesworth Press, Wakefield, West Yorkshire

This book is dedicated to the informal mentors I have had in recent years who have guided and supported me – giving me encouragement, support and opportunities both online and in person. Debbie Kidd, Rachel Lofthouse, Sam Twiselton and Jenny Webb – thank you.

Contents

Foreword by Professor Rachel Lofthouse iii

Foreword by Reuben Moore vii

Acknowledgements ix

Introduction 1
    About the focus groups – what makes a good mentor? 3

Chapter 1. Set high expectations 7
    Why is this standard important? What does the research say? 9
    Focus group findings 11
    How can I help my mentee meet this standard? 13
    Summary 20

Chapter 2. Promote good progress 23
    Why is this standard important? What does the research say? 25
    Focus group findings 28
    How can I help my mentee meet this standard? 29
    Summary 38

Chapter 3. Demonstrate good subject and curriculum knowledge 41
    Why is this standard important? What does the research say? 44
    Focus group findings 49
    How can I help my mentee meet this standard? 51
    Further reading – developing subject knowledge 60
    Summary 64

Chapter 4. Plan and teach well-structured lessons 67
    Why is this standard important? What does the research say? 70
    Focus group findings 78
    How can I help my mentee meet this standard? 79
    Summary 90

Chapter 5. Adapt teaching **93**

Why is this standard important? What does the research say? 95

Focus group findings 104

How can I help my mentee meet this standard? 106

Summary 112

Chapter 6. Make accurate and productive use of assessment **115**

Why is this standard important? What does the research say? 118

Focus group findings 123

How can I help my mentee meet this standard? 125

Summary 132

Chapter 7. Manage behaviour effectively **135**

Why is this standard important? What does the research say? 137

Focus group findings 145

How can I help my mentee meet this standard? 146

Summary 154

Chapter 8. Fulfil wider professional responsibilities **157**

Why is this standard important? What does the research say? 159

Focus group findings 164

How can I help my mentee meet this standard? 165

Summary 172

Bibliography 175

About the author 189

Foreword by Professor Rachel Lofthouse

No profession wants to lose its newest recruits before they have developed the confidence, wisdom and expertise to feel comfortable meeting the dynamic challenges of their workplace and are ready to lead and mentor colleagues and those still training. If the school sector is to sustain a diverse and expert workforce, education leaders and policy makers need to be aware of the knock-on effects that follow the loss of teachers early in their career. We cannot populate critical leadership roles with the very best teachers if those same teachers are now in management positions in retail or publishing, are working as freelance tutors, or have concluded that they cannot maintain positive personal and family lives while slogging up the career ladder.

Depending on which year you pick up this book, you will be able to look up the current teacher retention statistics. Perhaps one impact of the coronavirus pandemic will be more teachers holding on to their jobs for longer as the economy takes a hit. However, there has been a trend – and not only in the UK – for teacher retention in the first five years to be a problem. Some people argue that this is no different than in other employment sectors. They suggest that in the future most people will be serial job-swappers, building up a portfolio career over long working lives, and that as such we should worry less about retention and focus instead on ensuring there are always new trainees in the pipeline. But this overlooks the value of schools as multi-generational communities; the role of teaching 'elders' in passing on the tacit knowledge that underpins the profession; and the wisdom that is needed to enable complex, nuanced decision-making to benefit staff, learners, families and the wider communities which are intricately bound to our schools. All of these are compromised if teachers leave before they reach their full potential.

I have a personal bias which has threaded through my professional and academic life. I enjoyed learning to teach and I enjoyed working collaboratively with a range of expert colleagues during my PGCE and first few years in post. Not one of them was the perfect teacher, and they would be the first to admit it, and not one of them expected me to be, either. They were all advocates for the subject (in my case, geography), they actively engaged in subject communities and cared passionately that students gained a sense of purpose and achievement from learning geography. They were good people to be around and they each had a sense of humour and of perspective. They were my allies in the staffroom. They had my back and they pushed me forward. They appreciated the knowledge I had gained from my recent degree and they encouraged my creative thinking to support the success of the department. They trusted me to make decisions and were generous with their advice when sought. I made it through my first four years and then on to a second school as a head of department where I gained the opportunity to become a mentor. I was not a perfect mentor, but mentoring over the ensuing five years created a fertile space through which my own professional identity really evolved. As a teacher educator and researcher, understanding and developing mentoring and coaching has been a constant endeavour.

New teachers benefit from being offered the space to grow, reflect, continue to observe others and work collaboratively with colleagues. Mentoring is at its most powerful when it is built on positive personal relationships between novice teachers and those with more experience. Expert colleagues become good mentors (formally or informally) when they allow new teachers to test out their emerging identity and build their confidence through affirming their professional development and growth. Good mentors ensure new teachers recognise that they should never feel isolated and to be assured that help can always be found in the profession. Learning to teach and staying in teaching is necessarily a social process, and we need to look for ways to foreground this dimension in our work with new teachers.

So far, so good. Mentors matter and many teachers enjoy mentoring. However, not all mentoring creates a positive professional learning environment. We typically conflate being a good teacher with being a good mentor, and while they are not mutually exclusive, they are also not inevitable. Being an expert colleague who mentors early career teachers means being aware of how novices learn in and from complex workplaces. It also requires the creation of reflective and productive spaces in which current practical and urgent tasks and dilemmas can be grounded in a robust professional knowledge base and where beliefs and values can be shared and shaped.

Will the introduction of the Early Career Framework be the moment when mentoring lives up to its potential to transform the profession? My response is that we need to guard against this opportunity being missed. This requires that mentoring is not just a sticking plaster or another tick-box activity. Mentoring needs to be situated in a professional educational landscape in which new teachers and mentors challenge professional working practices that are restrictive, too often performative and sometimes even punitive (not to mention fractured, unforgivably busy and underfunded).

How do we do our best as expert colleagues to ensure that the early career years of those joining our profession are happy and rich in opportunities for professional development? We need to make sure that we do not dilute mentoring by assuming that anyone with adequate teaching experience can step into the role untrained or unsupported. We must not treat mentoring as the Cinderella role, done diligently on the sidelines of our core purpose as teachers and leaders, with few resources and little advocacy of its significance by those in more powerful positions. We must ensure that as professionals we treat professional learning seriously – we assume it is complex and know it is vital. If we get this right, enhanced mentoring could be the remaking of the profession.

Professor Rachel Lofthouse
Professor of Teacher Education and Director of CollectivED
Carnegie School of Education, Leeds Beckett University

Foreword by Reuben Moore

It is a real privilege to be able to write a foreword to such a valuable book for the sector. Supporting new teachers to have a strong start is critical to the profession itself and to the young people we serve. If colleagues do not have it, they are more likely to leave, they may struggle for longer than is necessary, they may burn out, or, at the very least, they may not pass on the best of their professional training and development to their pupils. Strong starts are critical.

Teaching is a complex business. Many try to simplify it and this can be useful up to a point. However, there is an issue of 'altitude' in the simplification. For example, we could simplify each move by a teacher in their interaction with pupils or materials, or even with concrete or defined actions. This will create a simple statement for each move but the 'list' could fill many books. If we choose a different altitude to keep it simple, we risk listing a few platitudes which are of limited use to new teachers planning lessons on a weekend. As a member of the advisory group that supported the development of the Early Career Framework, this was one of the challenges we had to wrestle with, along with a few others.

I recall that when I was a new teacher myself, I watched really experienced teachers who made it look simple. In fact, it sometimes looked like magic. By some magnificent sleight of hand, the teacher explained complex concepts that the pupils not only understood but could also manipulate and apply to new situations. Yet, in my early attempts in the classroom, this never seemed to work for me. Some of the differences lay in the time they had spent in honing that explanation over the years, the number of pupils they had taught, the expertise gained and the experience reflected upon. All of this mattered. Those expert teachers had thought deeply about their work, engaged with the research, and gained feedback from peers and other experts. They understood through their pupils' assessments what had been understood and what had not, and who was ready to move on and who was not. Therefore, being a good teacher takes time. If new colleagues starting out have to bear so many challenges until they have gained this knowledge, what happens if some give up before that day arrives? We know that many do withdraw before that day. Anyone's resilience would be severely tested if you felt that you were not getting better.

The Early Career Framework is an attempt to prevent this, to provide a precise research informed structure that gives a strong starting point for colleagues in their early years in the profession. It provides insights that encourage new teachers by making the chance of success in the early years of teaching more likely. Let us be clear, though: no one document or, indeed, book or piece of research can provide everything the new teacher needs in order to thrive quickly and become expert. However, we have to start somewhere; if we do not, then we are at risk of hindering a generation of colleagues in their support of our young people. The introduction to the Early Career Framework describes a minimum entitlement and this cannot be understated. The framework is not the entirety of what new teachers should learn. Expert educators in our schools and universities bolster this minimum entitlement significantly, but it is a concrete and defined starting point. The other thing to say is that some will read it and find little that is new – again, that is no mistake. We have some great places, people and opportunities for those early in their career to develop. However, the challenge is that access to these places, people or opportunities is not universal. Everyone deserves access to these development opportunities, not just those in the right places.

The Early Career Framework provides a guide, an entry point and an entitlement to colleagues in their early years in the profession so they can develop more quickly towards expertise than they would have done alone. Teaching is a team sport and therefore new colleagues should have the support of mentors and others in school and beyond to help; the Early Career Framework can make this support more precise and therefore more likely to be adopted into the new teachers' everyday work.

This book is such a valuable asset to any new teacher or their mentor, and Haili Hughes is a great guide to the framework. She has years of experience in schools both being supported by those who are more expert and also in leading the development of others. She also has an excellent insight into research through her own further study in her several master's degrees and current doctorate study. Haili guides us through the framework methodically, focusing on underpinning research while also gaining insight from new teachers about challenges and issues. She provides practical and evidence informed advice to sidestep those pitfalls identified in the findings. It is a really effective structure, as it is both practical and holistic. Haili brings her insights from numerous schools and settings, as well as what must be hundreds of interviews, to bear on this topic. It is done authentically, acknowledging the challenges of the role of a new teacher. The book succeeds in not making the reader feel like a failure, while at the same time demonstrating an ambitious bar for mentors to strive towards, which will in turn help our young people to achieve through great teaching by all colleagues.

Reuben Moore
Executive Director, Teach First

Acknowledgements

Thank you to all of the newly qualified teachers who took the time to speak to me about their experiences – both positive and negative. Understandably, many of them wished to remain anonymous due to the sensitive nature of what they were discussing. However, the following teachers were happy to be named: Daniel Bradish, Melissa Burfitt, Abby Camilleri, Selina Clarke, Gaby Coleman-Carey, Julia Di Mambro, Chloe Dodd, Natasha Froggatt, Elise Galvin, Susan Gee, Sam Green, Paige Mudge, Danielle Payton, Rebecca Powell, Neelam Rajput, Anuradha Sharma, Isabel Squires and Harpreet Virk.

Introduction

Speak to anybody who has left the profession after a few years and, more often than not, they will cite a lack of support as one of the reasons they felt unable to continue as a teacher. Mentoring matters – and a well-designed mentoring programme facilitated by a knowledgeable, enthusiastic mentor makes a massive difference to an early career teacher's feelings of success (Holloway, 2001). This is why the Early Career Framework (ECF) is one of the most exciting developments in education for many years as it promises a quality of support and provision for all early career teachers, which will no doubt help to reverse some of the worrying figures that see one in five teachers leave schools within two years (Weale, 2019). The ECF has improved the support package for new teachers by extending their funded training entitlement to a structured two-year package of high quality professional development.

As part of the government's drive to recruit and retain teachers, the framework aims to increase the resources and improve the opportunities that are open to early career teachers by providing a comprehensive entitlement to what new teachers will need to learn about and how to learn about it during those first crucial years. It contains sections on behaviour management, pedagogy, curriculum, assessment and professional behaviours, and is underpinned by academic research. In addition to the training materials and opportunities, new teachers will also be entitled to 5% of their time away from their classrooms to focus on their professional development, for which schools will receive funding. But perhaps most significant is the allocation of a dedicated mentor to advise, support and guide the new teacher, who will also receive training and professional development in order to help them fulfil their role successfully. There are several ways into the profession, whether that is through the traditional PGCE university route or through the school-centred initial teacher training provided by providers such as Teach First. This is why there are two forewords to this book, from Rachel and Reuben, who represent both routes and can vouch for the vital work contained within it.

I was lucky enough to be invited to one of the Department for Education's round tables when the policy was being refined and formulated, and I was inspired by the hard work, research and dedication which had gone into its creation. What became clear during this experience was how important mentors would be in supporting new teachers and that, more so than ever before, school leaders would need to acknowledge this and give them the necessary time to dedicate themselves fully to the role. The framework is clear and thorough and should complement the Teachers'

Standards (Department for Education, 2011) that the newly qualified teacher (NQT) has to evidence; they are not an extra job as they align so closely and support early career teachers in finding ways of meeting them. The framework, and the rationale for its formulation, can be found here: https://www.gov.uk/government/publications/early-career-framework.

Mentoring can be defined in many different ways: *Merriam-Webster's Ninth New Collegiate Dictionary* (1983) defines it as someone who is a wise and trusted teacher or counsellor, whereas Mentor Scout describe a mentor as someone who is willing to use their time and expertise to develop and guide another person who may be less experienced than them.[1] Mentors need to have certain qualities that can help their mentees to develop and flourish. Kerry and Mayes (1995) define some of these as the ability to nurture, to be a role model, to encourage and counsel, to focus on the mentee's professional development and to sustain a caring relationship over time. This is where the ECF comes into its own, as these essential qualities of a successful mentor are made explicit in the very nature of the recommendations of what new teachers should learn.

What is great about the standards in the ECF is that the 'Learn that' and 'Learn how to' criteria are all based on evidence informed research. Presently, it seems like there is a cultural and philosophical gulf between teachers and educational researchers, but this needn't be the case. It is important that teachers explore what research has to offer them, and the framework gives specific links for books and articles they can access to get them started. Of course, education is a polarising subject, filled with differing opinions on what constitutes 'good' teaching. This book is not an agreement or testament to these strategies and claims, and nor does it seek to diminish or decry the opinions of those who don't agree with them, but it is a clear and accessible guide on how mentors can use the research contained in the framework practically to help their mentee to develop and to meet the standards. What is more, it places mentors as the agent of change in their schools, as they are the 'expert colleagues' from whom new teachers can learn. With this power comes great responsibility, so I have used principles from the instructional coaching model to guide mentors in how best to support their mentees.

Instructional coaching has been in the spotlight recently, as it has shown promising results in schools, with a recent meta-analysis by Kraft et al. (2018) revealed positive effects of coaching on instructional practice. Furthermore, Gregory et al.'s (2016) qualitative evaluations revealed that it can help teachers to connect faraway, standards-based policy with their day-to-day teaching strategies. Instructional coaching suits the ECF perfectly as it is based around the idea of a teacher working

---

1   See https://www.mentorscout.com/mentor.cfm.

with another trained expert to help them learn, adopt new teaching practices and provide feedback, while combining teaching and content expertise. There is no standard coaching model for this approach, but Jim Knight's (2016) was particularly useful when writing the practical guidance in each chapter. The summing up section at the end of each chapter is also influenced by his ideas about teachers needing to collaborate with their mentors and learn from their expertise. It follows the principle that coaching is a cycle, with student engagement and learning at the centre of it. There needs to be time for planning and observations, as well as time to enact change and reflect at the end of it. In addition, success factors need to be specific, which is why this model works so well with the statements in each standard. Instructional coaches must also be knowledgeable and bring what Knight (2016) refers to as a research-based 'instructional playbook', so they can be the expert colleagues that this book refers to them as, who bring the best practice pedagogy into their schools and pass their expertise onto their mentees.

About the focus groups – what makes a good mentor?

To write this book, I conducted several different types of qualitative research as I was keen to see where mentoring may have previously gone wrong or to highlight where there had been successes from which new mentors could learn. Just over a hundred NQTs were interviewed in a mixture of telephone, online and in-person discussions on their experiences of being mentored and how their needs had been met in relation to the competencies detailed in each standard. Their answers were illuminating and really helped to guide the practical advice for mentors in each section. One of the questions asked was about what makes a successful mentor, and some of the results have been published here as a basis for mentors to work from in defining their role and also as a glorious celebration of what a rewarding job it can be.

First and foremost a mentor has to be approachable. If a mentor isn't approachable then, as an NQT in a new school and new role, I would not have the confidence to do basic things such as ask questions to expand my knowledge but also take risks. There have been times this year where I went to my mentor and said, 'I have an idea – it is either going to be brilliant or completely flop, but I'm going to give it a try.' The only reason I felt I could do this on an observation was because I knew if it went badly then my mentor and I had a good enough professional relationship to address it in such a way that I can learn.

Having a 'good' mentor can make or break your teaching career. A good mentor is impartial, tries to limit subjectivity when analysing lessons and sets the expectations or targets prior to the lesson. For example, my NQT mentor and I used Rosenshine's principles (2012) to guide our lesson observations, and feedback sessions were delivered in a coaching style. This opened up the conversation to positive and constructive discussion, which I think a lot of trainees would benefit from.

[A good mentor] has an attitude that everyone can improve their teaching – even them.

I've found that more experienced teachers make excellent mentors. Teachers with experience know the exam boards inside out, they've taught the texts numerous times and have more of an insight into what works and what doesn't work. That's not to say that a young mentor wouldn't be as successful, but I feel that they just don't have the same knowledge/experience of pedagogy. It needs to be someone who is genuinely passionate about teaching (the last thing an NQT needs is someone who has lost all passion and enthusiasm for teaching and who radiates negativity).

A mentor should not ask you to do something they wouldn't be prepared to do themselves. Equally, they should prompt you with questions that make you think, rather than just give you the answers.

Someone with time – everyone is busy, but if the mentor has dedicated and demarcated time to mentor, then as the mentee this helps you not to feel guilty for using up more of their precious time.

I believe that a good mentor will not just have the subject-specific knowledge and experience in the classroom to help with those more tricky/challenging scenarios, but they also have to be an approachable person. If your mentor isn't approachable and compassionate, then how will you be able to build a confident foundation in seeking advice and constructive criticism? Even being able to come and vent at the end of a stressful day, or getting them to come and observe to give advice, this is something that stems from that initial relationship.

A good mentor remembers how overwhelming it can be to enter the world of teaching and helps the new teacher to navigate their own way through with success. A good mentor needs to recognise where the new teacher is at the beginning and throughout, all the time asking: what skills do they have that they can make good use of to build up their confidence? What situations/settings/interactions do they need to experience more of in order to better understand how a good teacher could respond? Anecdotally, from my fellow trainees, I think very often where the mentor–trainee relationship falls down is when the mentor is too aggressive or prescriptive in trying to mould the new teacher into exactly their vision of a good teacher, a mimic of themselves, taking the agency away from the new teacher.

This sounds cheesy but a good mentor acts like your mini cheerleader! This doesn't mean that they unequivocally praise you, but they give you that little boost to build your confidence.

If you have never been a mentor before, becoming one can seem quite a daunting task: it is a great responsibility and can take up a large amount of time and energy when done correctly. You may meet with your mentee formally once a week, but you will need to be available at all times to offer support and guidance or to answer any questions the NQT may have. There are also times when you will need to offer a supportive listening ear or help in formulating action plans to develop them professionally. That is why this book uses the phrase 'expert colleague', which is taken from the framework itself. A mentor needs to have the experience to draw on to be able to advise a new teacher, and they need to be an expert in their field so that they can model best practice and impart their wisdom to those who are new to the profession. Expert colleagues also embody the resilience that new teachers need if they wish to remain in education because they have weathered many storms and possess the tenacity required to enjoy a long career as a teacher. This is why it is so important that mentors are experienced teachers who have much to offer those entering the world of education.

Even if you have been a mentor previously, the new ECF offers something wholly different from what has guided the practice of mentors previously, which is why there is a need for this book. Each chapter is based on a standard from the framework and begins by exploring the research which underpins the guidance – a sort of detailed literature review which is thorough but accessible. The chapters then give a summary of findings from the focus groups which link to the standard discussed, complete with quotations from participants which can help to guide mentors in what they should and should not do. This leads on to a section which draws on both the research and focus group findings together to give practical advice and guidance for activities, reading and strategies that mentors can try with their early career teacher.

The advice and guidance in this book does not focus simply on developing new teachers; it also develops experienced teachers through their role as a mentor, encouraging them to become reflective practitioners and improve their own practice. With this in mind, each chapter ends with a summary model. This not only adopts some of the principles of instructional coaching, such as creating an action plan, having the chance to put learning into practice and an opportunity for evaluation and next steps; it also includes a section on collaboration, which stresses the importance of mentors working together with NQTs to model best practice and develop their own knowledge and pedagogy.

This book does not claim to be a panacea for the problem of how best to mentor, but it does offer busy teachers a practical interpretation of the ECF in order to support new teachers and guide and inspire them in this vital role.

Chapter 1
Set high expectations

High Expectations (Standard 1 – Set high expectations)	
Learn that ...	**Learn how to ...**
1. Teachers have the ability to affect and improve the wellbeing, motivation and behaviour of their pupils. 2. Teachers are key role models who can influence the attitudes, values and behaviours of their pupils. 3. Teacher expectations can affect pupil outcomes; setting goals that challenge and stretch pupils is essential. 4. Setting clear expectations can help to communicate shared values that improve classroom and school culture. 5. A culture of mutual trust and respect supports effective relationships.	**Communicate a belief in the academic potential of all pupils, by:** • *Using intentional and consistent language that promotes challenge and aspiration.* • *Setting tasks that stretch pupils, but which are achievable, within a challenging curriculum.* • *Creating a positive environment where making mistakes and learning from them and the need for effort and perseverance are part of the daily routine.* • *Seeking opportunities to engage parents and carers in the education of their children (e.g. proactively highlighting successes).*

High Expectations (Standard 1 – Set high expectations)	
Learn that ...	**Learn how to ...**
6. High quality teaching has a long-term positive effect on pupils' life chances, particularly for children from disadvantaged backgrounds.	**Demonstrate consistently high behavioural expectations, by:** • *Creating a culture of respect and trust in the classroom that supports all pupils to succeed (e.g. by modelling the types of courteous behaviour expected of pupils).* • *Teaching and rigorously maintaining clear behavioural expectations (e.g. for contributions, volume level and concentration).* • *Applying rules, sanctions and rewards in line with school policy, escalating behaviour incidents as appropriate.* • *Acknowledging and praising pupil effort and emphasising progress being made.*

Notes

Learn that ... statements are informed by the best available educational research.

Learn how to ... statements are drawn from the wider evidence base including both academic research and additional guidance from expert practitioners.

Why is this standard important?
What does the research say?

The research area of teacher perceptions and the effect they could have on pupils is an important area to study as it could have far-reaching effects on individuals and have a substantial impact on pupils' future lives. (Hamilton, 2006: 208)

Teachers' expectations about their students and the potential of what they can achieve – or, indeed, the way they are capable of behaving – can have a substantial impact on their learning, progress and emotional wellbeing. Often, teacher expectations are formed from our own constructs of belief, which can be difficult to quantify as they are sometimes implied and rarely made explicit. They are made up of teachers' cultural, biographical and professional identities, which all inform their perceptions of their students' abilities (Rushton, 2011). These perceptions can have far-reaching consequences in the classroom, as they can impact on teaching and learning decisions (McNair, 1979; Pajares, 1992; Bullough and Baughman, 1997). This could suggest that some teachers may not teach more challenging concepts to those they perceive to be less able or may have lower expectations for their behaviour.

Previous research has also revealed that these perceptions are constructed in a casual way, with decisions being made about students' potential with little real guidance or evidence (Hoge and Cudmore, 1986). These concepts of who is intelligent and who isn't exist powerfully in teacher perceptions and are evident in their actions. They can be seen as a 'folk pedagogy' (Torff, 1999: 196) and can create a cascade effect, which can have substantial effects not only in the classroom but can also impact on further education choices and career choices in later life (Sternberg, 1990). For instance, I have vivid memories of my careers advisor at school laughing at me when I told him about my ambitions to go to university and work as a national newspaper journalist. He clearly didn't think that my working class, council estate background could stretch that far.

But it isn't as simple as just class or socio-economic status. The stereotypes that form teacher perceptions can come from a range of different experiences, including student characteristics and how these are perceived by staff. These preconceptions of potential can be reinforced by a school's performance levels and then become self-fulfilling (Bradbury, 2011). Recent initiatives in schools, such as focusing on students with minority ethnic backgrounds, on low incomes or in receipt of the pupil premium, may contribute to teacher perceptions that these students have less potential and are less capable, meaning educators may lower their expectations (Campbell, 2015). In addition to teachers' personal experiences, stories in the media about particular groups of students may influence teachers' perceptions of their characteristics, attributes and abilities. Earp (2010) studied stereotype activation and the way that teachers may behave as a consequence of this. He concluded that teachers who are unaware of these intrinsic biases may see them as stemming from their students' performances rather than from their own stereotypes.

Research has also demonstrated that the kinds of language used in both direct and indirect exchanges with students in the classroom can have a profound effect on their motivation and aspiration. Weinstein (2002) identified that some teachers in their study differentiated in their interactions with high and low expectation students. These teachers clearly moderated their language when giving instructions to those they perceived to be high or low ability students. They communicated performance goals differently and, due to this, some students felt that their teachers had lower expectations of them than their higher ability peers.

Although this research could make rather grim reading, there is a ray of hope: it is fundamentally clear that teachers and the expectations they have of their students, and their potential to achieve, can make a huge difference. Therefore, it is vital that expectations are always high and that they see the academic potential in all students. Teacher quality is so important, and quality first teaching is what makes the biggest difference to pupil outcomes (EEF, 2018d).

Behaviour in the classroom could also be a significant factor when improving teaching quality. Disruptive behaviour is a major factor in why new teachers leave the profession (McInerney, 2018), and 43% of participants in the Education Support Partnership's *Teacher Wellbeing Index 2018* said they had suffered from mental health problems, which they attributed to dealing with constant behaviour problems at school. Building strategies for instilling positive behaviour for learning is an essential part of training to teach. Obviously, habits and routines which instil positive behaviour traits enable students to engage in learning, which ensure they can make good academic progress: instead of spending time tackling constant low level disruption, teachers are freed up to concentrate on providing better teaching. It also models to students how they can sustain good relationships with both adults and their peers through behaving in an acceptable way. Establishing these kinds of behaviour habits will not only help students to learn better in school, but will also give them smoother transitions into college, employment and adult life, as they will understand how society works.

Focus group findings

Some may argue that teachers should naturally have a belief in the academic potential of all students, and of course most do. Yet, with the approach of setting by ability being prevalent in most schools and some exams still being tiered, this belief can sometimes be hard for teachers to communicate successfully to students. The early career teachers questioned felt that their mentors were mostly supportive when it came to behaviour: instead of focusing on the negative interactions when it came to disrupted learning, they helped to guide solid behaviour management strategies which were underpinned by the school's behaviour policy and academic theory.

One participant spoke about how their mentor had reframed the behaviour struggles to take out the emotional element of dealing with them and reminded them that it wasn't personal – it was about maximising learning. They said: 'I worked in a school catering to an area with students from diverse backgrounds, abilities and personal contexts. The focus in discussions was always about how best to support the student(s) with their learning. The professionally framed approach to all scenarios highlighted that the focus should always be on the progress of the student(s) and that this should remain the core of every choice in and outside of the classroom.' The participant spoke warmly about this experience, as in a previous school they had witnessed other mentors being quite prejudiced about certain groups or classes, which came through in their suggestions about how to manage their behaviour and made the trainee teacher feel even more anxious.

Some in the group felt that their mentor had struggled with how best to support them with behaviour; other than coming into their lessons and 'taking over', they felt that there hadn't been any really fundamental support. One teacher spoke about a difficult Year 10 class where they had students who refused to sit down and kept leaving the classroom whenever they wanted, and when they were in the classroom they shouted out and threw things across the room. As their mentor was on their planning, preparation and assessment (PPA) time when the teacher taught this class, they often popped in to see how things were going, but they did this so often that the students started to make jokes about it, which made the situation worse. Although the mentor was trying to be supportive, the new teacher felt that this just emphasised the point that they were unable to cope with the class and the students also saw it as a weakness. It seemed that the mentor was out of their depth, as they had only been teaching for a year, so the early career teacher wished they had a more experienced mentor.

However, another teacher at a challenging school in special measures could not speak highly enough of the support they had received when a Year 11 student pushed them in the corridor: 'The head teacher came down on the pupil like a ton of bricks and I got an apology. I felt truly supported and valued, while also feeling confident that the student would not do it again.'

Less time was spent on guiding the early career teachers in how to communicate their belief in the academic potential of all students; it was just expected that they would intrinsically know how to do it, and some participants questioned felt that they would have benefited from succinct instruction. One teacher spoke of how they had found themselves teaching two classes in the same year group, where one was higher ability than the other. They detailed how they had found themselves 'dumbing down' the content for one class, because before meeting the class, their mentor had described them as 'weak', which coloured their perceptions about what the students were capable of doing. This resulted in the teacher experiencing some disruptive behaviour in the class, as the students were bored and felt uninspired and unchallenged. When they discussed it with their mentor, they were told, 'That's just the way they are!' Another teacher told a more positive story about how their mentor had modelled positive language in the classroom and had observed how they 'taught to the top' in their lessons and then scaffolded down for those who needed it. Being able to see a more experienced teacher doing this had helped the trainee to do this in their own lessons, and subsequently they felt that embedding challenge for all levels and abilities was one of their strengths.

How can I help my mentee meet this standard?

One of the key words to instil in your mentees is consistency. As we know, young people are surprising creatures of habit: they like to walk into a classroom and know that things are going to be the same as they were yesterday and the day before. They don't want to feel disarmed. Hence the use of whole school behaviour policies; a classroom where teachers just do what they like and allow students to 'get away' with low-level disruption, just to keep the peace, makes it much more difficult for them and other colleagues to teach. It can result in chaos. But how can NQTs create an environment that is built on uniform responses to behaviour choices, so that students are able to understand expectations and make positive choices?

To start, it is important that the new teacher fully understands the school's behaviour policy – it is about much more than just reading it. Even the clearest and most straightforward of policies have their nuances and can be interpreted differently by staff. Recently, I was in a continuing professional development (CPD) session where we focused on what the school's behaviour policy meant in practice. The staff were given scenarios by the assistant head in charge of behaviour and, after hearing them, had to go and stand next to the sign which displayed the consequence they would have given the child. There was not a single scenario where all staff agreed on a consequence. In the quest for consistency this poses a huge problem. It is important that there are no shades of grey and that policies are followed to the letter. Obviously, teachers need to use their emotional intelligence and consider the underlying causes for the negative behaviour of their students, but this can be done later, after the behaviour has been diffused. Perhaps having a coaching conversation with your mentee and going through possible scenarios with them might provoke some interesting discussions about how they would react to negative student behaviour. Not only would this empower them to realise that they can control their own learning environment, but it would also give them the confidence to know that they have weapons in their arsenal that they will not be afraid to use. Forewarned is forearmed.

Many schools have warning systems, such as a verbal, note in diary or written warning, before a formal record of negative behaviour is given. This can be one of the most inconsistent rules to implement in a classroom, as sometimes it just seems easier to gloss over small instances of disruption rather than stop the lesson to give warnings. This is why simple solutions such as writing names on a notepad where you can record positives and negatives throughout the lesson work so well. Using a notepad rather than the board will avoid there being an element of competition where students vie to become top of the bad behaviour league table, seeing comments or ticks as a badge of honour. Also, having a notepad handy can remind you to jot down the names of students who deserve positive praise and recognition for their efforts, so you can later contact home or record their names on your school system. After all, it is important to be consistent in recording exemplary behaviour as well as negative. This will earn your trainee a huge amount of respect, which is so important in building up those vital relationships between students, teachers and parents.

Respect is vital and students need to be modelled courteous and friendly behaviour by their teachers. After a tough day, it is easy to let your feelings and exhaustion show. I have been guilty of it myself. One day, I had been through a sleepless night with a toddler and had what seemed to be a grim succession of challenging lessons. By period 6, I was officially fed up and when I dragged myself outside my classroom door to reluctantly meet and greet my Year 10 class, the annoyance with life must have shown on my face. The first boy to arrive said, 'Oh no, you're in a mood.' I was mortified and asked him how he could tell. He responded with, 'Miss, your face don't lie and I can always tell whether the lesson is going to be good or bad by your face.' This really upset me, and I vowed never to create a negative atmosphere for the students again – regardless of what the rest of my day had been like.

One of the ways you can support your mentee to do this is by making sure they are fully prepared to begin purposefully when they teach their classes for the first time. Make some time to sit down with them and create some seating plans. As a mentor who has worked at the school for a while, you will probably know the students; if you haven't taught them before, it is helpful to ask colleagues in your department for a couple of lines about each of them – who they work best with, any issues you need to be aware of, even students not to sit next to each other! Of course, using prior data on students is great for making sure there is opportunity for differentiation when creating the new teacher's seating plan, but practical tips from colleagues who know the students are worth their weight in gold. It is also worth remembering not to stress out your NQT or cause more anxiety by revealing that classes are particularly difficult. As a trainee, I have vivid memories of my old mentor looking at my timetable and revealing to me that the class I was going to teach are a 'total nightmare' and even wishing me 'Good luck getting them to do anything!' Not only does this worry an already anxious new practitioner, but it also colours their perceptions of the young people they are about to meet. Comments like this can be a trigger for implicit bias – whether we acknowledge it or not.

Another key way to help your NQT to foster a mutual relationship of respect in their classroom is by advising them to spend some time in the first lesson setting out the ground rules with students; it is absolutely imperative that they start on a purposeful and calm note and establish basic boundaries for their class. Advise your trainee to engage the students in the creation of the rules and boundaries; in this way, they are much more likely to engage with and abide by them. One way of doing this is to encourage your mentee to display descriptions of several disruptive behaviours on the board and ask the students to make a list of things they could do to curb those behaviours. Doing it in this way means there is a focus on the positive, and the students are more focused on the solution rather than dwelling on the behaviour itself.

Observations and team teaching are a valuable tool in helping your NQT to create a purposeful working environment and to manage behaviour in their own classrooms. You need to model how to create a relationship of mutual respect with the students you teach and demonstrate practical ways this can be done by your NQT. One important facet is to always be present during the lesson. This sounds obvious, but juggling workload as a new teacher can be tough, so it is tempting to sit at your computer and get on with paperwork or planning while the students are completing independent tasks. Circulating around the room during the lesson shows the students you are available to support and help them when needed or to give them some encouragement along the way. If the new teacher sees you doing this, they can see for themselves that this is a better approach. If you can invite your NQT to watch your lesson, with a focus on how the students respond to the caring but firm manner you use in your own classroom, you could then discuss what the effects of this are in a meeting after the lesson. It is important to remember that teachers all have different approaches and ways of working, and that you are not trying to create a carbon copy of yourself. However, while your mentee is finding their own 'teacher voice' and style, it can be useful for them to observe the strategies used in an experienced practitioner's classroom and what works for them.

For some new teachers, it can be difficult to strike the balance between being authoritative and being friendly with students, particularly if they are a very young teacher in secondary who is only a few years older than their Year 11 students. As a new teacher in my late twenties, I fell into this trap with my first GCSE class and ended up paying the price for it. I inherited a top set who were sparky and hilarious and, of course, I wanted them to like me. I became a bit too matey and informal, making quips and sometimes resorting to sarcasm to get a laugh as I believed this meant I had them 'on side'. If you notice your trainee falling into this trap, you could direct them to read *Boys Don't Try?* by Matt Pinkett and Mark Roberts (2019). Their chapter on relationships has some brilliant comments on sarcasm in particular and mentions its 'pernicious effects', which can sometimes seem cruel and as if the teacher is targeting individual students. Furthermore, it creates a negative tone to the lesson which hardly inspires the students to try their best and create high quality work.

Behaviour management is a crucial part of learning to teach; the way students behave is strongly correlated with the outcomes they will eventually achieve in school. Better behaviour equals more learning and the opportunity for students to achieve more academically (Bennett, 2017). Of course, the curriculum also needs to be challenging, so there is scope during every lesson for students to build on prior knowledge and for them to feel stimulated and energised to try more difficult tasks. But building an environment of stretch and challenge in a classroom takes time and it is something you will have to support your NQT with throughout the two years of mentoring. It begins with your mentee recognising that learning should be difficult and that students may not quickly or automatically 'get' the content they are teaching. It can be really difficult to embrace these tough moments – the silence when they ask a question or when they need to re-explain a concept in a different way. However, if young teachers do not accept that these moments are part and parcel of teaching, they risk underestimating their students and end up placing a metaphorical limit on what they can grasp and achieve.

In order to embed challenge and articulate to all students that they believe they can succeed, NQTs will first need to know their students well enough to be able to plan the sorts of activities and content that will stretch them academically. This can be extremely difficult at the beginning of the school year as all there may be to work with is hard data from assessment points during the previous year. Your department might want to consider using a separate book for assessments during the school year, which students can take with them as they move through the school. This will show their progress and will also be a useful record to hand over to the next teacher. In this way, less time is wasted at the beginning of the school year, as they will be well informed about each student's strengths and areas for development. This would really help new teachers to understand their students and plan accordingly. In addition, it would be beneficial to meet with your NQT before the end of the summer term and create a spreadsheet for each class in which general targets could be collated to inform planning. You could even assist them in beginning to create a folder of useful starter activities to target these weaker areas, so that they have some resources already planned before school starts in September. Not only will this take the pressure off your NQT but it will also give them a sense of ownership. Many departments already have pre-prepared curriculum resources and lessons that all teachers in the department use, but the opportunity for a new teacher to plan more bespoke activities for their own classes is a good foundation for creating medium-term plans later in the academic year.

Learning intentions are one of the most important ways that teachers can communicate to their students that they are *all* expected to think deeply and critically and that there will be no coasting or completing the bare minimum. For this reason, I would advocate not advising an NQT to use differentiated lesson objectives such as 'some', 'most' and 'all'. Through bitter experience, I have also learned that if some students are given the opportunity to take the easy option, they will take it, believing that you are intimating that only 'some' are capable of reaching the top. They can also take up half a lesson to read – time which could have been spent more productively by ascertaining prior knowledge or starting to learn key terminology which will be used later on in the lesson. What is more, learning intentions and objectives can be vague and abstract, so if you can spend some time with your mentee modelling how to formulate strong enquiry questions rather than objectives, this will not only help them to plan lessons that respond to this question, but it will also firmly anchor the students' learning, giving them a sense of accomplishment that they are able to respond to the question after this series of learning. As Dylan Wiliam and Siobhan Leahy (2015) assert, if students are clear about where their learning journey is going and what it is leading to, they are much more likely to take responsibility for it. The use of questions, rather than objectives, will give them a deeper sense of completion and personal achievement.

Essentially, if the aim is to create a positive atmosphere, where perseverance, resilience and learning from mistakes is the norm, you need to encourage your NQT to use their planning to give students mastery learning skills – although this can be challenging. Students need to have the confidence to draw on subject-specific strategies and prior knowledge, so they can then use these to complete tasks and move their learning forward. Research from the Education Endowment Foundation (EEF) states that, on average, mastery learning approaches lead to an additional five months' progress, so it is well worth spending some of your meeting time together supporting the new teacher in understanding how to use these strategies. A good start would be to direct them to independently read the EEF's evidence summary on mastery learning.[1] You could then come together and discuss the report's findings and use their Teaching and Learning Toolkit to collaboratively plan a series of lessons where these strategies are embedded over a half term. At the end of the series of lessons, there should be time for reflection and next steps, where the impact on attitudes to learning from the students can be evaluated.

Another way that students can be stretched and challenged is through the employment of skilful teacher questioning, where new teachers try to avoid being over-reliant on what Robin Alexander (2008) terms the standard initiation-response-feedback (or IRF) model. The problem with this system and its use in the classroom is that a large proportion of students can sit back and be bystanders rather than participators in the learning. Instead, you could explore different questioning techniques together with your NQT and trial some of them with both of your classes. The aim is to encourage every student to make a contribution and think deeply about their learning. Even teaching students how to construct their own questions in your subject will help with

---

1   See https://educationendowmentfoundation.org.uk/public/files/Toolkit/complete/EEF-Teaching-Learning-Toolkit-October-2018.pdf.

this. Alex Quigley (2012) has come up with some brilliant suggestions for different types of questioning that you could both trial in your classrooms and later discuss their impact. It is always useful and interesting to produce an initial audit of the kinds of questions you both actually use in lessons – the results are sometimes surprising! You may find that you are stuck in a rut yourself with questioning and it may be useful for your mentee to see this. We are all developing; nobody is the finished article. It is great for them to realise that you are both developing in your roles and learning together.

In addition, it is important that teachers model the kind of scholarly and academic language they expect their students to use, which will also promote challenge and aspiration. Part of this is about ensuring that academic vocabulary in their subject is taught specifically and schemes of work are planned with disciplinary literacy principles in mind. The National Literacy Trust website (www.literacytrust.org.uk) provides a wealth of information and some great resources, and it is well worth attending one of their courses or webinars to get some practical advice on how to help new teachers to embed these principles across the curriculum. In *Teach Like a Champion 2.0* (2015), Doug Lemov talks about ways to improve students' language skills through his 'Right is Right' strategy. This ensures that students realise that their work will not be completely finished until they have developed their answers fully, using academic vocabulary and a range of thoroughly explained examples. Helping your NQT to have the confidence to model this via visualisers or on the interactive whiteboard will really give students an idea of the standard of work they will be expected to complete. Also, teaching them how to give students the opportunity to rehearse and redraft their thinking both in written work and orally will lead to more sophisticated thinking.

Finally, one of the things that new teachers are most nervous about is contacting parents and carers. This is a shame as they can be one of the most effective tools in engaging students in their education. Often, there is a stigma around parents that they can be unsupportive or too challenging, but this may be because often they are only contacted about the negative interactions their children have in school. No doubt, there is a department or whole school policy of rewards, whereby postcards are sent home or students are given credits or something similar, that your NQT could utilise to start to build these relationships. However, there are other ways that a classroom teacher can engage with parents to celebrate successes, such as weekly email bulletins. The initial set-up can be time-consuming, but once you have shown them how to create email groups, the emails will only take five minutes to send at the end of the week. Parents are busy and a quick message detailing what their child has learned this week in your NQT's lesson, along with a 'well done' for any successes, can be a huge motivator to students, while also empowering parents to feel more involved and knowledgeable.

Chapter 1: Summary

Identify goal:
To set high expectations by communicating a belief in the academic potential of all students by demonstrating consistently high behavioural expectations and emphasising progress being made.

Evaluate and reflect on the standard:
- Are there any aspects of behaviour that the NQT is still struggling with? What steps can be put in place to develop this?
- Ask them to rate their confidence in questioning and having high expectations. Identify areas where they need more support. Create an action plan for further reading and next steps to develop their skills.

Standard
1 – Set high
expectations

Apply the learning:
- Explore various scenarios of negative behaviour during your coaching conversations and ask your mentee how they would deal with them.
- Formulate some descriptions of disruptive behaviour together which the NQT could use with the class to encourage them to come up with their own rules.
- Provide opportunities for the new teacher to observe you, with a focus on how you are 'present' during the lesson and how you create a positive learning environment.
- Both trial different types of questioning in your lessons and reflect on how engagement has improved in both of your lessons.

Come up with a plan:

- Ensure that the school's behaviour policy is clearly understood by the NQT and that positive behaviour is rewarded as consistently as negative behaviour is pointed out.
- Remind them to model positive and courteous behaviour at all times.
- Help to create seating plans and assist in arranging meetings with students' previous teachers to collect richer data than just assessment grades.
- Show them how to foster a relationship of mutual respect with firm but fair boundaries from the first lesson, where expectations are made clear from the start.
- Ensure that they include enquiry questions and mastery techniques in lesson plans.
- Show them how to set up email groups for parents in each class for easy communication.
- Buy a visualiser for them and model how it can be used in lessons.

Learn together:

- Read the chapter on relationships in *Boys Don't Try?* by Matt Pinkett and Mark Roberts (2019) and keep a diary of self-reflection for a day on how you both implemented some of the strategies.
- Create a bank of useful starter activities together which build on prior knowledge of the students based on targets collated from former teachers.
- Individually read the EEF's evidence summary on mastery learning (EEF, 2018e) and come together to discuss the findings, using their Teaching and Learning Toolkit to collaboratively plan a series of lessons where these strategies are embedded over a half term.
- Read Alex Quigley's (2012) blog post on questioning and complete an audit of the kinds of questions you both use in lesson to help you develop more strategies.

Chapter 2

Promote good progress

How pupils learn (Standard 2 – Promote good progress)	
Learn that ...	**Learn how to ...**
1. Learning involves a lasting change in pupils' capabilities or understanding. 2. Prior knowledge plays an important role in how pupils learn; committing some key facts to their long-term memory is likely to help pupils learn more complex ideas. 3. An important factor in learning is memory, which can be thought of as comprising two elements: working memory and long-term memory. 4. Working memory is where information that is being actively processed is held, but its capacity is limited and can be overloaded. 5. Long-term memory can be considered as a store of knowledge that changes as pupils learn by integrating new ideas with existing knowledge.	**Avoid overloading working memory, by:** • *Taking into account pupils' prior knowledge when planning how much new information to introduce.* • *Breaking complex material into smaller steps (e.g. using partially completed examples to focus pupils on the specific steps).* • *Reducing distractions that take attention away from what is being taught (e.g. keeping the complexity of a task to a minimum, so that attention is focused on the content).* **Build on pupils' prior knowledge, by:** • *Identifying possible misconceptions and planning how to prevent these forming.* • *Linking what pupils already know to what is being taught (e.g. explaining how new content builds on what is already known).*

How pupils learn (Standard 2 – Promote good progress)

Learn that ...	Learn how to ...
6. Where prior knowledge is weak, pupils are more likely to develop misconceptions, particularly if new ideas are introduced too quickly.	• *Sequencing lessons so that pupils secure foundational knowledge before encountering more complex content.*
7. Regular purposeful practice of what has previously been taught can help consolidate material and help pupils remember what they have learned.	• *Encouraging pupils to share emerging understanding and points of confusion so that misconceptions can be addressed.*
8. Requiring pupils to retrieve information from memory, and spacing practice so that pupils revisit ideas after a gap are also likely to strengthen recall.	**Increase likelihood of material being retained, by:** • *Balancing exposition, repetition, practice and retrieval of critical knowledge and skills.* • *Planning regular review and practice of key ideas and concepts over time.*
9. Worked examples that take pupils through each step of a new process are also likely to support pupils to learn.	• *Designing practice, generation and retrieval tasks that provide just enough support so that pupils experience a high success rate when attempting challenging work.* • *Increasing challenge with practice and retrieval as knowledge becomes more secure (e.g. by removing scaffolding, lengthening spacing or introducing interacting elements).*

Notes

Learn that ... statements are informed by the best available educational research.

Learn how to ... statements are drawn from a wider evidence base including both academic research and additional guidance from expert practitioners.

Why is this standard important?
What does the research say?

Cognitive load theory and the principles of metacognition, where educators explore how students learn, has been at the forefront of educational research and theory for the last decade. When I trained to teach in the early 2000s, my PGCE course barely focused on the science behind learning, yet now the principles of cognitive load theory, working memory and how to avoid overloading working memory are bed-rocks of teacher education. First coined by psychologist John Sweller in the 1980s, cognitive load theory is based on a model of how our memory works and how we process and retain new information.

Cognitive load theory proposes that our working memory, which processes the tasks we are doing, is only capable of dealing with a limited amount of information at any one time. For every task we do, there is an amount of information processing and effort which takes place called the cognitive load. Sweller et al. (2011) break this down into three different categories: intrinsic, extraneous and germane.

Intrinsic cognitive load refers to the difficulty of the material or task; a student's prior knowledge of the topic being studied can also have an impact on this. An example might be a Year 6 student who knows how to recognise and use complex sentences, who is later asked in Year 7 to begin to analyse the impact of sentences in the text. They have previously built schemata which will help them to complete this task, whereas for a younger student the intrinsic load may be too onerous. It is all relative. This is why ascertaining prior knowledge is so vital.

Extraneous cognitive load refers to the distractions and disruptions in the working environment. This could include the way the material being learned is presented or any external aspect which does not support effective learning. Consider overcrowded PowerPoint slides or classrooms which are smothered in brightly coloured posters that catch the eye to the point of distraction. The effort the student expends in digesting the things that are imposed on their working memory may overload it and, crucially, take some of the effort away from the task itself.

Germane cognitive load is about how information is actually processed and how schema (a cognitive framework or concept that helps us to organise and interpret information) are constructed and developed. Here, the strategies a learner uses to learn and organise material come to the fore. Opportunities to enhance consolida-tion and retrieval, which are both processed by our working memory, aim to optimise the germane load.

Overall, the theory suggests that if, during our learning episodes, our cognitive load exceeds our capacity to process new information, it will be difficult to complete activities successfully. When summarised in these simple terms, it is easy to see why Dylan Wiliam named cognitive load theory as 'the single most important thing for teachers to know' (Wiliam, 2017b). Instead of constantly breaching the boundaries of the limited capacity in students' short-term working memory, we should be aiming to reduce the cognitive load so they are able to process and move the knowledge to their long-term memory – whose capacity is much greater. Unfortunately, if students have an incorrect or incomplete grasp of the subject knowledge, they will be unable to draw on previous knowledge in their long-term memory and their working memory may once again become overloaded.

Research by Susan Gathercole (Gathercole and Pickering, 2000; Jarvis and Gathercole, 2003; Gathercole and Alloway, 2008) reveals that the majority of students who exhibit the signs of poor working memory are slower to make progress and learn in areas such as reading, mathematics and science, both in primary and secondary school. They are simply unable to meet the memory requirements of the task they are doing, and the crucial information they need to complete a sentence, activity or task is lost. This means they are unable to see the task through to a successful conclusion unless they are able to re-access the information they need. If this information is not stored in a schema in their long-term memory, they may have to guess and risk errors or abandon the task completely. This can result in missed learning opportunities which will lead to delayed learning if these episodes occur frequently. Previously, teachers may have just labelled these children as 'lazy' or 'daydreamers' – we have all experienced learners who spend more time staring out of the window rather than completing their work. Indeed, recent evidence has concluded that this is a typical sign of a student with working memory problems (Kane et al., 2007) which can no longer cope with the demanding cognitive activities that are being required of it. There will be lots of strategies later in this chapter to help your NQT to manage cognitive load, which draw on academic research but are rooted in practical classroom activities.

To optimise the germane load, it is important to activate students' prior knowledge, so that links can be made between what they already know and how it links or can be built on by new knowledge. This means that students can then create more robust schema and use them for information retrieval in the future. Hattie and Yates (2014) regard prior knowledge as being one of the most influential factors when it comes to learning. However, in the classroom, recall and applying prior knowledge to new learning can be a complex task for some students and will require support from teachers. Sometimes students struggle to make connections between what they already know and new information, so as Howard-Jones et al. (2018) observe, it is important that students are prompted to dig deep and recall prior knowledge before they are given new information. Of course, it is vital that the prior knowledge is accurate: it can support learning when it is correct but will hinder knowledge if it isn't.

The aim is to move students towards becoming experts in your subject. Rana and Burgin (2017) claim that experts are able to draw on a range of efficient problem-solving strategies and recognise patterns in their learning that novices are unable to do, because they have developed more elaborate schema. The challenge for teachers is not only to attempt to engage each child in activating their prior knowledge, but also to quality assess their understanding so that any misconceptions that are elucidated can be corrected. If teachers are aware of the way their students learn, and of strategies they can use to maximise the likelihood that they will retain knowledge, they will be promoting good progress in their classes.

Of course, cognitive load theory is not the only important theory that teachers need to know about in order to understand the way students learn. There are also social factors, as outlined in Vygotsky's (1978) zone of proximal development, and economic factors, such as Bourdieu's theories of reproduction (Bourdieu and Passeron, 1977), which examine issues of class, socio-economic background and cultural capital. Oracy is also incredibly important: Hattie (2012) found that teaching strategies which prioritised high quality student talk produced the biggest effect sizes. There are so many factors about how students learn that need to be acknowledged, but the scope of this book is not comprehensive enough to give a full overview of every one of them. Besides, that may be a little overwhelming for both a mentor and a new teacher anyway! Cognitive load theory is the primary focus of this chapter because 'the implications of working memory limitations on instructional design can hardly be overestimated … any instructional design that flouts or merely ignores working memory limitations inevitably is deficient' (Sweller et al., 1998: 252–253).

As teachers, we have all been in those CPD sessions where the content has been whizzed through and we feel we have been left with little to remember and take away. I am sure we have also all been in sessions where what we are hearing is so complex that we leave more confused than when we entered. If we are having these moments as well-educated adults, then the students we teach must be too. Cognitive load theory helps us to understand why we may feel like this and what we can do as teachers to make sure that we avoid this happening to our students and can instead maximise learning opportunities. The ECF refers to a number of the principles of cognitive load theory; in other words, from a research perspective, it is seen as one of the bedrocks on which successful teachers build their lesson design. As this book is based on the ECF document, it is important that cognitive load theory is central to its recommendations, although I also acknowledge that there are other considerations in learning that new teachers can explore later on in their career.

Focus group findings

Many of the newly and recently qualified teachers I spoke to as part of my research felt that their school had prioritised CPD and supported reading focused on metacognition and the concepts of cognitive load theory, because senior leaders had recognised that its principles underpin curriculum choices. This included ideas for how to structure lessons, with models promoted that included starter activities that established students' existing understanding and previous lesson content, which were then reviewed at the end of the lesson. There was an expectation that all lessons would be structured in this way, as the gaps in the students' knowledge at the end of the lesson would then feed into the teacher's future planning. The participants felt supported by this structure but sometimes felt that it was restrictive, as lessons sometimes ran over or naturally took a different direction.

Some of the NQTs in primary had been encouraged by their mentor to meet their new class' teacher from the previous year. They felt that this was excellent practice as they were able to get practical context from a fellow professional who knew the pupils really well. Although they had been given data, some teachers felt overwhelmed and confused about what the data showed and how they could use it, so talking about each child's prior learning allowed them to prepare adequately. It was felt that meeting the previous class teacher also helped with the logistics of activating prior knowledge, as one participant recalled: 'Their reception teacher was able to tell me what phonics videos the class had watched and were used to. So now, before I introduce a new sound in phonics, I often show the class a video they watched in reception – to recap, but also I find it a helpful tool to show them how far they've progressed.' This also made the new teachers feel more confident about collaborating as they had made that initial contact and felt more like they were part of the team.

Participants also told me about the subject-specific support they had received when being advised on how not to overload working memory. In English, an NQT had received advice from their mentor about how to chunk texts – particularly the dense 19th century novels in English literature that a less able class were struggling to understand: 'We worked with the chunking method, or boxing method, which is to read a certain chunk and then answer some comprehension questions and look at some exam-style questions for that, and to then move on to the next paragraph when they have understood that part, until they have read the complete piece.' Their mentor then modelled how they could ask the students in subsequent lessons to summarise what they had learned in three to five bullet points, so they could quickly gauge their understanding and how much knowledge they had retained. They felt that this guidance had really helped them to understand how the students could best learn.

However, some early career teachers felt they hadn't received any clear or specific guidance on metacognition, or cognitive load theory in particular, but had heard it mentioned in passing during other CPD sessions. Ironically, colleagues who were running the CPD had assumed that they had prior knowledge of the theories so they didn't need to go over the concept! One participant spoke of their panic every time it was mentioned and said that they felt 'too embarrassed' to ask now as they had nodded along at other CPD sessions and pretended they knew what the facilitator was talking about. They thought that it would have benefited them more for their schools to have assumed that they were starting from scratch sometimes, but to also provide links to articles and books that they could dip into and read more about a strategy or topic.

A few of the NQTs questioned felt that when it came to them trying to understand how students actually learn, they had received little guidance. One claimed, 'It is just something that teachers and schools don't tend to think about and is just taken for granted that they do.' Their mentor had told them that it didn't really matter as long as the students were getting on with their work and could pass exams. This left the new teacher feeling really frustrated as they then felt silly for asking. This is clearly something that needs to be improved in schools, because understanding how students learn is vital when it comes to planning appropriate learning materials.

How can I help my mentee meet this standard?

First and foremost, it is important that your mentee is aware of cognitive load theory and how working memory can be overloaded. As we have seen from the focus group findings, early career teachers may not have a good understanding of the concepts mentioned in Standard 2 of the ECF, so it is important not to take it for granted; we would not make this assumption with our students, so we should not do so for new teachers. The Chartered College of Teaching has published several straightforward and thorough articles on these topics which make a great and easily digestible starting point (see Shibli and West, 2018; Tay, 2018).

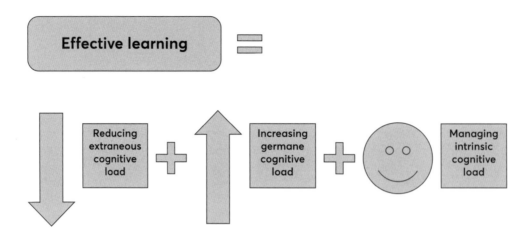

Figure 2.1. Effective learning (adapted from Sweller, 2010)

The key to effective learning is to reduce the extraneous cognitive load and increase the germane, while also trying to manage the intrinsic (see Figure 2.1). There are quick fixes and small changes that will help your mentee do this easily in their own classroom. One of them is to rethink their classroom displays. I am certainly not a minimalist and my classroom reflects this! The walls were always resplendent with motivational quotes and key information, and the display boards were heaving with examples of student work. But some research from Fisher et al. (2014) made me rethink this: they suggest that classroom displays are not only distracting but may even be detrimental to children's learning. In their study, students were less likely to stay focused, and even ended up attaining lower test scores, when they had lessons in a heavily decorated classroom, as opposed to a sparser one. There was also a correlation between the amount of time they were distracted, which suggests that there is a significant relationship between these two variables. However, there is a caveat: there was significantly less disruption after the children in the study got more used to the displays in the second week. Didau (2015) comments that this is probably the point at which the display had become meaningless wallpaper, although the intention of most displays is to capture students' attention.

A few years ago, it seemed that Ofsted were keen on having students' work on display and it was something they were looking out for during inspections. I remember feverish late nights putting up backing paper and borders in the corridors on the evening before a visit. Now, some schools have eschewed displaying student work at all. The Michaela Community School in London famously doesn't display work because the head, Katharine Birbalsingh, thinks that the time it takes for students to make it and teachers to put it up isn't worth the small benefit it delivers (Didau, 2015). Author and English teacher Carl Hendrick (2015) has also written about the dubious educational value of motivational posters. He asserts that although the sentiment behind changing students' self-perception is a noble one, the messages on posters are often a form of 'soft psychology' and promote 'a culture that privileges the media-soundbite over critical reflection'. Essentially, there are ways of improving the growth mindset of students which will have more of an impact than a poster telling them to 'reach for the stars'.

Of course, this doesn't mean that you need to advise your mentee to leave their classroom completely undecorated; personalising your classroom is one of the great rites of passage when becoming a teacher. It is just about being more strategic. A well-decorated classroom in which the students' successes are celebrated is lovely, but the colours and what is on the displays should be chosen judiciously in order to prevent any overt distractions. In their book *Think It – Map It*, Ian Harris and Oliver Caviglioli (2003) describe some of the more effective uses of classroom displays, starting with model map displays, which they claim inspire students and are a great revision tool. Figures 2.2–2.4 show some examples of these principles in action.

Figure 2.2. Example of a 'calm' classroom in Birmingham

Figures 2.3 and 2.4. Fe Brewer's displays at Rawlins Academy in Leicestershire

A summary report by the University of Salford, *Clever Classrooms*, found that classroom displays 'should be designed to provide a lively sense to the classroom, but without becoming chaotic. As a rule of thumb 20–50% of the available wall space should be kept clear' (Barrett et al., 2015: 35). Less is more when it comes to avoiding extraneous cognitive overload. Consider advising your mentee to have displays only at the back of the room which they can refer to during the lesson and to leave the sides of the classroom free from clutter. Even bright colours and wiggly borders can be distracting, so perhaps stick to calmer, pastel colours and avoid borders altogether.

Resources are another important factor to consider. Extraneous cognitive load can be reduced by the way in which we present instructions: a lack of clarity in our instructions will put too high a load on working memory. Students will then spend too much time trying to work out what the instructions are and how to do the task, as opposed to developing their schema. It is vital to model what PowerPoint presentations should look like, so your mentee doesn't fill them with excessive writing and overload the students with information. Oliver Caviglioli (2015) suggests that PowerPoint presentations are often boring because they are more of an aide-memoire to keep the presenter on track rather than for the audience. He recommends that teachers devote only one point to each slide and that it should be expressed as a phrase or short sentence, with an image placed behind it that resonates with the message being presented. This can be particularly difficult for new teachers who sometimes use PowerPoints as a security blanket. Caviglioli's guide on how to decide what to include in PowerPoint presentations is very helpful, so perhaps you could use this to collaboratively plan and create a lesson resource with your mentee.

Promoting good progress is irrevocably intertwined with classroom pedagogy and quality teaching. This includes learning activities and lesson sequencing and ensuring that there is an opportunity for retrieval practice and the review and practice of key ideas and concepts. Breaking down complex ideas into small chunks in a knowledge organiser is an excellent way to help students build secure foundational knowledge before they are introduced to more complex content. Encourage your mentee to produce some knowledge organisers which you can reflect on together to see how easy they are to digest. Frederick Reif (2008: 128) argues that 'teachers should attempt to develop explicitly, and then gradually expand, a well-organized knowledge structure that students can actively use. In this way, a student's knowledge can be well organized at every stage and can be gradually reorganized as more knowledge is acquired.' This reduces the risk of cognitive overload as students acquire new knowledge bit by bit and can make sense of it in terms of making connections between the things they will learn. The information in a knowledge organiser should contain the answers to simple 'why' and 'how' questions and can be organised or categorised into groups. Again, Caviglioli's brilliant book *Dual Coding with Teachers* (2019a) sets out easy guidelines for how to organise a plethora of classroom resources, including knowledge organisers and posters. His message is to cut out unnecessary information, chunk information together, signal hierarchy with font size, keep everything aligned, and use restraint – resist the urge to add more or superfluous colour and images. You could use this checklist in your meetings to reflect on resources your mentee has produced.

Not only do knowledge organisers provide a knowledge foundation for students, they also make it much easier for teachers to produce tasks and quizzes which will quickly assess how much students know and what they need to revisit and revise. Quizzes at the beginning of lessons, such as quick sixes (quick six-question recall quizzes), can be really effective ways of assessing prior knowledge and also addressing misconceptions, as students can share which answers they got wrong and the reasons why this might have happened. There are many variations on this type of activity which work well across the key stages and curriculum. Figures 2.5–2.7 provide some examples of tools designed to establish students' prior knowledge. Although these are subject specific, they could be easily adapted for almost any curriculum area. These can then be used or repeated at various intervals so that spaces between initial exposition and recall are elongated. In English, this might be exemplified by the class doing a quiz on Act 1, Scene 3 of *Macbeth*, when Macbeth initially meets the witches, when the class are beginning to read a scene later on in the play when he revisits them again. This gives students the opportunity to delve into their long-term memory and connect the dots with the contextual information they have learned previously (see pages 35–36).

Beware that knowledge organisers can be misused as simply a memory tool; in order for them to be utilised successfully, a distinction needs to be drawn between memory and understanding. According to John Biggs, students approach their learning in one of two ways: either aiming to memorise as much as possible, which may lead to only a surface understanding, or with the wish to understand the material in a deeper way. Biggs (1987: 343) states that when using the deeper approach, 'a student has the intention to understand. Information may be remembered, but this is viewed as an almost unintentional by-product.' Clearly, memory is important, but it is understanding that leads to a memory of the material being formed. A combined approach is more beneficial, therefore, with knowledge organisers used to help understanding as well as an aide-memoire for revision and the encoding of key concepts and chunks of information.

Climate Change

Work with your partner to come up with a mind map to show what you know about climate change. You can use a whole page.

Copy and complete the following into your book. You might want to add your own categories.

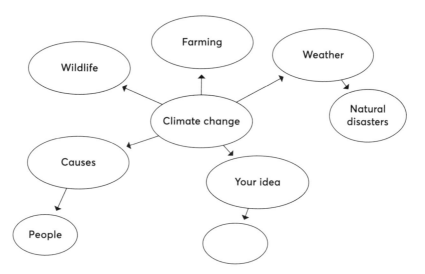

Now come up with seven to ten questions that you would like to explore. Two examples are given below.

1. What effect does climate change have on health?

2. Aside from people, what else causes climate change?

Write them in your book, leaving some lines between each one so you can write in the answers when you find them out.

Figure 2.5. Establishing prior knowledge – geography

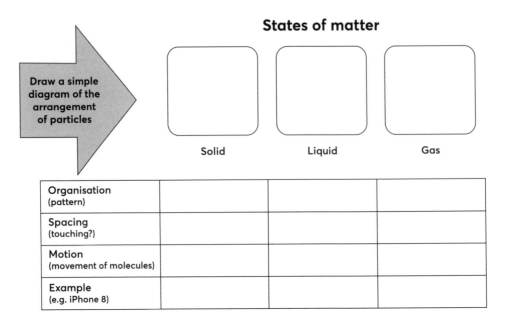

States of matter

	Solid	Liquid	Gas
Organisation (pattern)			
Spacing (touching?)			
Motion (movement of molecules)			
Example (e.g. iPhone 8)			

Figure 2.6. Establishing prior knowledge – science

Success criteria	Proof
I can factorise a quadratic expression in the form $x^2 + bx + c$ (grade 6).	Factorise $x^2 + 7x + 10$
I can recognise the difference between two squares and know how to factorise them (grade 7).	Factorise $x^2 - 81$
I can factorise a quadratic expression with a negative coefficient of x^2 (grade 7).	Factorise $-x^2 - 2x + 15$
I can factorise quadratic expressions in the form $ax^2 + bx + c$ (grade 7).	Factorise $3x^2 + 10x + 7$

Figure 2.7. Establishing prior knowledge – maths

When supporting a new teacher to implement some of these strategies, the power of guided or collaborative planning and team teaching cannot be underestimated. By opening a learning dialogue between you and your mentee, where you can research and explore ideas for learning activities together, you will learn alongside them and also improve your own pedagogy. It is crucial for an NQT to see that teachers are constantly reflecting and developing, and that leaders learn too.

Once prior knowledge has been established and the exposition of any new theories or information has been imparted, it is necessary for the students to have the opportunity to practise their new knowledge and skills in activities in which they are able to have some success. This is vital because once the challenge is increased, and their knowledge becomes more secure, the scaffolds can be taken away and students will be confident that they are able to attempt the tasks. In my own subject, English, those scaffolds may take the form of exemplar responses, models of how to analyse language effectively, or even work on the visualiser. It is important, however, that the scaffolds demonstrate how to structure answers but don't give away the answers. Tasks shouldn't be easy; taking away the element of challenge will not only bore students but will also stall progress. This can be a fine balancing act, particularly if the teacher feels that the class are struggling with the concepts they are teaching. However, if you can encourage your mentee to keep including the repetition of key concepts, retrieval and practice opportunities in their lessons, the students' confidence will improve and the NQT will be rewarded when they experience the best thing about teaching: the light bulb moment for their students.

Chapter 2: Summary

Identify goal:
To promote good student progress by avoiding overloading working memory, building on students' prior knowledge and increasing the likelihood of students retaining material.

Standard 2 – Promote good progress

Evaluate and reflect on the standard:
- Does the NQT now feel confident that they understand the principles of cognitive load theory and how it impacts on their planning and teaching?
- Ask them to rate their confidence and identify areas where they need more support.
- Create an action plan for further reading and next steps to develop their skills.

Apply the learning:
- Ask your mentee to bring some resources such as knowledge organisers and PowerPoint slides to the lesson and reflect on their suitability, using Caviglioli's (2019a) checklists.
- Do some team teaching of retrieval practice activities.
- Encourage your mentee to observe experienced colleagues across the curriculum, with a focus on how they build on students' prior knowledge and increase challenge. They can then trial similar activities and strategies in their own classroom.

Come up with a plan:
- Use the principles of cognitive load theory to show the NQT the best way to decorate their classroom and produce lesson resources.
- Help them to plan and deliver lessons that include opportunities for retrieval practice, scaffolding for challenge (which can be taken away later) and to practise new skills and knowledge.

Learn together:
- Explore cognitive load theory by reading the articles in the Chartered College's *Impact* magazine (Howard-Jones et al., 2018; Shibli and West, 2018; Tay, 2018) and research from Fisher et al. (2014) on classroom displays together.
- Both read the *Clever Classrooms* research (Barrett et al., 2015) and discuss the findings and how they could be related to your own context.
- Collaboratively produce a guide on making resources for the department based on Caviglioli's *Dual Coding with Teachers* (2019a). This can be shared with colleagues at a department meeting.

Chapter 3

Demonstrate good subject and curriculum knowledge

Subject and curriculum (Standard 3 – Demonstrate good subject and curriculum knowledge)	
Learn that …	**Learn how to …**
1. A school's curriculum enables it to set out its vision for the knowledge, skills and values that its pupils will learn, encompassing the national curriculum within a coherent wider vision for successful learning. 2. Secure subject knowledge helps teachers to motivate pupils and teach effectively. 3. Ensuring pupils master foundational concepts and knowledge before moving on is likely to build pupils' confidence and help them succeed.	**Deliver a carefully sequenced and coherent curriculum, by:** • *Identifying essential concepts, knowledge, skills and principles of the subject and providing opportunity for all pupils to learn and master these critical components.* • *Ensuring pupils' thinking is focused on key ideas within the subject.* • *Working with experienced colleagues to accumulate and refine a collection of powerful analogies, illustrations, examples, explanations and demonstrations.*

Subject and curriculum (Standard 3 – Demonstrate good subject and curriculum knowledge)

Learn that ...	Learn how to ...
4. Anticipating common misconceptions within particular subjects is also an important aspect of curricular knowledge; working closely with colleagues to develop an understanding of likely misconceptions is valuable. 5. Explicitly teaching pupils the knowledge and skills they need to succeed within particular subject areas is beneficial. 6. In order for pupils to think critically, they must have a secure understanding of knowledge within the subject area they are being asked to think critically about. 7. In all subject areas, pupils learn new ideas by linking those ideas to existing knowledge, organising this knowledge into increasingly complex mental models (or 'schemata'); carefully sequencing teaching to facilitate this process is important. 8. Pupils are likely to struggle to transfer what has been learnt in one discipline to a new or unfamiliar context.	• *Using resources and materials aligned with the school curriculum (e.g. textbooks or shared resources designed by experienced colleagues that carefully sequence content).* • *Being aware of common misconceptions and discussing with experienced colleagues how to help pupils master important concepts.* **Support pupils to build increasingly complex mental models, by:** • *Discussing curriculum design with experienced colleagues and balancing exposition, repetition, practice of critical skills and knowledge.* • *Revisiting the big ideas of the subject over time and teaching key concepts through a range of examples.* • *Drawing explicit links between new content and the core concepts and principles in the subject.* **Develop fluency, by:** • *Providing tasks that support pupils to learn key ideas securely (e.g. quizzing pupils so they develop fluency with times tables).* • *Using retrieval and spaced practice to build automatic recall of key knowledge.*

Subject and curriculum (Standard 3 – Demonstrate good subject and curriculum knowledge)	
Learn that …	**Learn how to …**
9. To access the curriculum, early literacy provides fundamental knowledge; reading comprises two elements: word reading and language comprehension; systematic synthetic phonics is the most effective approach for teaching pupils to decode. 10. Every teacher can improve pupils' literacy, including by explicitly teaching reading, writing and oral language skills specific to individual disciplines.	**Help pupils apply knowledge and skills to other contexts, by:** • *Ensuring pupils have relevant domain-specific knowledge, especially when being asked to think critically within a subject.* • *Interleaving concrete and abstract examples, slowly withdrawing concrete examples and drawing attention to the underlying structure of problems.* **Develop pupils' literacy, by:** • *Demonstrating a clear understanding of systematic synthetic phonics, particularly if teaching early reading and spelling.* • *Supporting younger pupils to become fluent readers and to write fluently and legibly.* • *Teaching unfamiliar vocabulary explicitly and planning for pupils to be repeatedly exposed to high-utility and high-frequency vocabulary in what is taught.* • *Modelling reading comprehension by asking questions, making predictions, and summarising when reading.* • *Promoting reading for pleasure (e.g. by using a range of whole class reading approaches and regularly reading high quality texts to children).*

Subject and curriculum (Standard 3 – Demonstrate good subject and curriculum knowledge)	
Learn that …	**Learn how to …**
	• *Modelling and requiring high quality oral language, recognising that spoken language underpins the development of reading and writing (e.g. requiring pupils to respond to questions in full sentences, making use of relevant technical vocabulary).* • *Teaching different forms of writing by modelling planning, drafting and editing.*

Notes

Learn that … statements are informed by the best available educational research.

Learn how to … statements are drawn from a wider evidence base including both academic research and additional guidance from expert practitioners.

Why is this standard important? What does the research say?

Every school and teaching practitioner has their own concept and ideas about what makes a good teacher and what great teaching is. The Sutton Trust report *What Makes Great Teaching?* (Coe et al., 2014: 3) defines it as 'that which leads to improved student achievement using outcomes that matter to their future success'. This may seem a bit limiting to some, as it implies that a teacher's skills and expertise are judged on the students' exam results. However, 'outcomes' does not have to refer just to exams; it can also be about fostering a love for learning and developing a confidence in the classroom or learning environment, which will stay with them after they leave education. In the same report, Coe et al. sum up the six key areas on which the research suggests the quality of teaching should be assessed: (pedagogical) content knowledge, the quality of instruction, classroom climate, classroom management, teacher beliefs and professional behaviours. These measures are discussed in other chapters, but this standard focuses on subject and curriculum knowledge, which actually has one of the strongest impacts on student progress.

It is no surprise that the subject knowledge of a teacher is of the utmost importance – after all, the love of our own subject and the aim of passing our passion on to a new generation is probably what has inspired us to become teachers! The research also backs this up: several studies have uncovered a relationship between a teacher's subject knowledge and progress made by students. For example, Sadler et al. (2013) tested science teachers on their own understanding of the content they were teaching and the misconceptions demonstrated by students. Overall, there was a positive relationship between teachers' understanding and students' understanding. In addition, Hill et al. (2005) cite a number of studies where it was found that teachers' levels of understanding and knowledge in mathematics had an effect on how well the students learned. In their study, they discovered that teachers who received a low score on their 'content knowledge for teaching' test had associations with almost a month's less learning for the students. However, it is also clear from the recent boom in education publishing that teachers are keen to develop themselves and their subject knowledge; just a simple search online or in any bookshop will reveal hundreds of subject-specific books written by teachers, academics and consultants that teachers can use to improve any possible part of their pedagogy.

But it is not just about devouring books and journals, as Timperley (2008: 19) states: 'to establish a firm foundation for improved student outcomes, teachers must integrate their knowledge about the curriculum, and about how to teach it effectively'. Therefore, teachers need to demonstrate their subject knowledge by identifying the key concepts in their subject that the students need to know and providing opportunities, through a knowledge-rich curriculum, for students to learn and master them. Understandably, curriculum has been top of the agenda over the last couple of years, with much of the focus in educational research focusing on how to build a secure and robust curriculum – one which motivates students and helps teachers to teach effectively. In addition, curriculum became a tenet of the new Ofsted framework, which then also catalysed many schools to reflect on their own curriculums and how coherent they were. In the framework guidance published in 2019, Ofsted stressed the importance of the sequence of the curriculum by stressing that 'The sequence of lessons, *not* an individual lesson, is the unit of assessment' (Ofsted, 2019: 9). Therefore, when the inspectors came into schools, they would be evaluating where the lesson they observed sat within a series of lessons and how teachers understood this. This also led to a shift away from the traditional grading of individual lessons to one of 'deep diving' into the bigger picture.

Consequently, the sequencing of the curriculum has been discussed and debated more than it possibly ever has been by middle and senior leaders, with the aim of creating a learning journey that is temporal and has movement. Christine Counsell (2018) has written about the curriculum being like a narrative, where 'every bit of content has a function'. For any narrative to make sense, we need to be able to remember what has come before and all the multiple strands of the story we have digested. It is the same with learning. Counsell uses the analogy of a narrative for learning because she believes that good curriculum sequencing should be 'constantly unifying, pulling things together so that they function'. In other words, building on prior knowledge, helping students to make connections and imbuing new content with meaning via the information they already have stored in their long-term memory.

But what kind of activities and strategies does evidence informed practice tell us are the most effective in doing this? One of the most popular methods of instruction among educators is Rosenshine's principles of instruction. Rosenshine originally published the principles in 2012, where he summarised the best part of half a century's worth of research on effective instruction and how teachers can best maximise its impact. The basis of his ideas comes from studies which observed teacher behaviours in the classroom and how this correlated with higher student outcomes. Experimental evidence was then explored for each of the principles, which suggested that if new teachers were encouraged to use and adopt these principles in their own teaching, it could result in better student outcomes.

More recently, Tom Sherrington published an excellent book, *Rosenshine's Principles in Action* (2019), which contains Rosenshine's original paper in the second half of the book and in the first part demonstrates how the principles can be put into practice in everyday classrooms. The principles are:

- Begin a lesson with a short review of previous learning.
- Present new material in small steps, with the opportunity for students to practise after each step.
- Ask a large number of students questions to gauge understanding.
- Provide students with models and worked examples.
- Provide opportunities for students to complete guided practice.
- Constantly check for student understanding.
- Obtain a high success rate.
- Provide scaffolds for difficult tasks.

- Provide opportunities for students to do independent practice and monitor this.
- Engage the students in both weekly and monthly reviews.

More experienced practitioners may look at this list and think they seem pretty obvious, and that they do them on a regular basis in most of their lessons. However, if we reflect deeply this may not really be the case. How many of us, for instance, ensure that our students obtain a high success rate of around 80% *and* balance the building of confidence with more meaningful, challenging tasks? I am not sure I do! Sometimes it is useful to reflect on the quality of your instruction, no matter how experienced you are.

Undoubtedly, using these principles, which align so well with cognitive science, will help students to build more complex mental models, as they will get to revisit the big ideas and concepts in their learning and make links between new content and core concepts continuously. Yet, Rosenshine's principles are not the only vision of what excellence in teaching looks like. There are many other theoretical frameworks and principles that teachers could follow which would result in improved outcomes too.

Unfortunately, the scope of this book is not wide enough to explore all of them. However, it may be useful to consider Danielson's Framework for Teaching, which appears in his *Enhancing Professional Practice* (2007), as an alternative to Rosenshine. The framework aims to provide a common language for instructional practice, while also offering a roadmap of practices which support great teaching across every career phase. It assesses four dimensions of teaching: planning and preparation, classroom environment, instruction, and professional responsibilities. It takes a more constructivist approach, recognising that a learner's understanding and knowledge is based in part on their own experiences prior to starting school. Unlike Rosenshine, Danielson doesn't give direct advice about what teachers should do; instead, he categorises certain practices that are judged to be more conducive to learning. Both the principles and the framework could be seen as more traditional than progressive, and good teachers are likely to vary their practice and methodology depending on the class or context and over the course of their career. What is important for an early career teacher, however, is that they have firm foundations based on evidence and research as a bedrock on which they can then build their own pedagogical style. As Hattie (2012: 84) suggests, 'The major message is that rather than recommending a particular teaching method, teachers need to be evaluators of the effect of the methods that they choose.'

For other voices in education, the curriculum should not be focused solely on the attainment of GCSE results-based outcomes, but also on encouraging a shared exploration of knowledge, which Debra Kidd calls 'grand narratives of learning' in her book *Curriculum of Hope* (2020: 8). She advises school leaders to refocus and consider the value of what is being taught and how it leads to lines of enquiry for children, who are then empowered to shape their future communities. I think great teaching does both of these things – it empowers and inspires, while equipping students with the knowledge, expertise and skills they will need in order to navigate the world and have a successful future. Despite the divisive bickering on Twitter about 'trad' versus 'prog' teachers, and sweeping generalisations about what they stand for, the truth of the matter is that most educators are somewhere in the middle and, what is more, this will change due to context, class and time of career.

One component which is key to demonstrating good subject and curriculum knowledge, no matter what side of the educational fence you sit on, is the need for teachers to help develop students' literacy. In his foreword to the EEF's *Improving Literacy in Secondary Schools* guidance report, Kevan Collins sets out the stark reality: 'Young people who leave school without good literacy skills are held back at every stage of life. Their outcomes are poorer on almost every measure, from health and wellbeing, to employment and finance' (EEF, 2019: 4). Secondary school teachers may have previously taken it for granted that students will arrive at school able to read well and write fluently, but this is not always the case. Primary colleagues put an enormous amount of work into phonics programmes, teaching unfamiliar vocabulary and beginning to foster a love of reading in pupils. When they get to secondary school, it may sometimes seem that literacy is something that is then forgotten about and only referred to in English lessons. The EEF's guidance challenges the notion that 'literacy in secondary school is solely the preserve of English teachers'[1] and recommends instead that disciplinary literacy should be prioritised across the curriculum. This includes providing targeted vocabulary and subject-specific academic language to students and teachers and prioritising tier 2 and 3 vocabulary in their teaching.

The report also stresses that students should be given the opportunity to read more complex academic texts, combining the reading with writing instruction which will help to improve the quality of students' extended writing. The use of models and exemplars is also recommended: students should be taught to recognise the features of high quality academic writing so they are able to emulate it in their own. In addition, this may give the feedback that teachers provide on students' work more credence, as they would be able to see that their teachers are trying to help them achieve a similar standard to the writing they have analysed together.

According to Rich et al. (2017), when a teacher corrects a common misconception, it needs to be believed for it to be effective. In an experiment, they assessed how participants responded to a refutation alone and a refutation with a supporting

---

1   See https://educationendowmentfoundation.org.uk/tools/guidance-reports/improving-literacy-in-secondary-schools.

explanation. They then rated their belief in the validity of the feedback. The participants came back a week later and once again rated the validity of the misconceptions; they found that participants corrected their misconceptions more often when they believed the corrective feedback. Therefore, a teacher who is knowledgeable and uses exemplars will be trusted by their students to give them appropriate feedback. In addition, participants corrected their misconceptions more often when they had received feedback with a supporting explanation. Skilful, regular feedback by teachers is key to the effective correction of misconceptions.

Focus group findings

Some of the NQTs interviewed experienced little opportunity to get involved in curriculum planning within their department. As a consequence, they felt that everything had already been planned or decided on before they started, or that they were seen as too inexperienced to contribute. This is a real pity as some of the freshest ideas I have encountered in the last few years have come from new entrants to the profession. It is true that new teachers need to work with more experienced colleagues to identify the essential concepts, knowledge and skills needed in a curriculum and to have ideas modelled about how to refine and collate the kinds of strategies needed to support students in lessons. However, it should be exactly that: a collaboration and a team effort.

One of the teachers in the focus group spoke about how they sat in on a co-planning day with two more experienced colleagues as part of their induction and helped to plan and sequence a scheme of work for the autumn term. They spoke about how helpful this was as it enabled them to see how the classes worked, as well as giving them ideas and boosting their confidence for when they would have to work more independently. Another explained how they had attempted to contribute ideas when the new curriculum was being planned and had found their suggestions shouted down and dismissed. This made them more reticent to get involved in the future as they had been made to feel that they had little to offer.

Another felt lucky that the department were particularly invested in developing the curriculum as a team, and they were all involved in choosing carefully selected literacy resources. The same participant spoke highly of the departmental CPD they had received on developing literacy, such as teaching vocabulary in a science setting and how to use the Frayer model (a graphical organiser used for word analysis and vocabulary building). The department also had very detailed schemes of work for both Key Stage 3 and 4 to which everybody was encouraged to make contributions and improve at the end of each teaching sequence. They remarked: 'This is invaluable as a new teacher – if you follow the scheme, you can't go wrong. I also think a department and a mentor that has the attitude that we can all improve all the time, not just new teachers, is important.' They felt that this avoided there being a two-tier system where only certain people's opinions were valued. Another participant added that if new teachers need experience to be able to write schemes of work, then if they aren't given chances and opportunities they would never develop the expertise required.

Alas, this sense of collective learning is not universal. A teacher in the group talked about their experience on a placement where the department had demonstrated much more of a closed mindset and were of the attitude that all of the experienced teachers in the department had nothing left to change or learn, and the early career teacher had to prove themselves to be accepted in the department. They recalled: 'I can imagine many trainees would have run away and never come back as the department was so hostile! I definitely think it is about the whole department and not just the mentor.'

There was a consensus that it is helpful in the initial months of teaching to have well-developed schemes of work that are written by more expert colleagues, which can then be tailored gradually for certain classes by a new teacher as they gain in experience and confidence. In much the same way as we guide the work of students, newer teachers appreciated a finished model to scaffold their understanding of what medium-term plans and lesson sequencing should look like. One of the participants added: 'During this time, as I was still not completely confident in my own abilities, I would discuss any changes I made to the learning sequences with my mentor; she would ask me questions around assessment and impact that would help me come to my own conclusions. My mentor was open to my suggestions and actively encouraged them.' Another of the teachers I interviewed had started at a school where there were no schemes of learning and teachers planned their own lessons based on a shared outcome at the end of the half term. They recalled that while this was great for autonomy and creativity, it was very stressful. The new teacher said, 'I had no idea whether I was doing the right thing as I had nothing to guide me. It was also really tough to fit making lessons and resources from scratch alongside everything else I had to do.'

Some participants felt incredibly supported not just by their mentor but also felt that the rest of the school supported them in their development. This took the form of focused observations, team teaching or tutorials on software used for literacy. This accessibility and willingness to lend a hand was really appreciated and made new teachers feel supported and part of the team.

How can I help my mentee meet this standard?

An early conversation in your meetings needs to have as its focus what is actually meant by a carefully sequenced and coherent curriculum. What does it look like? What should it include? Central to this discussion needs to be the tenet that what students are learning builds on what they have learned previously. Consequently, it is important to give the new teacher access to the curriculum map for the five or seven years that students are at the school, so they are able to explore the whole learning journey and how a year group develops from one academic year to the next in terms of knowledge and skills. A useful exercise might be to produce a ladder between Year 7 and 11 for a unit and to model how the skills are built from one topic to the next (see Figure 3.1). The new colleague can then go away and repeat this exercise for themselves with different units. This will give them a very visual representation of how carefully content is sequenced when planning a curriculum.

Vertical coherence is important: when reading down the ladder, it becomes clear where key concepts and skills are missing at lower levels that need to be developed for GCSE or SATs assessment objectives. Careful attention must be paid to how the material being studied is organised. Essentially, it is about getting your mentee to consider what students need to know, and how and when to teach them that skill or knowledge. If the teacher has never seen or read the national curriculum for the key stages they teach, this is a useful exercise: it is important that they are able to see how schools fit into a coherent national system. Also, the clear statements about what each student should be able to do by the end of the key stage are really helpful starting points for thinking about constructing long- and medium-term plans. An interesting exercise would be to identify where these skills are covered in your department's curriculum map. This would not only give the teacher a deeper understanding of the requirements in their subject area and see the connections between the lessons they are teaching and how they fit into the wider curriculum, but it would also empower them to suggest changes and improvements to existing schemes of work.

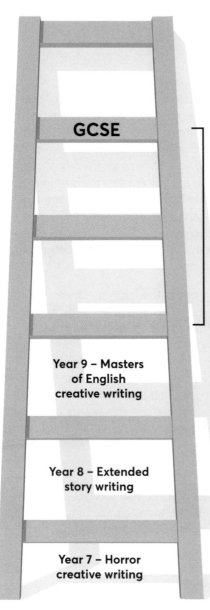

GCSE

AO5 skills:

- Communicating clearly, effectively and imaginatively, selecting and adapting tone, style and register for different forms, purposes and audiences.

- Organising information and ideas, using structural and grammatical features to support coherence and cohesion of texts.

AO6 skills:

- Candidates must use a range of vocabulary and sentence structures for clarity, purpose and effect, with accurate spelling and punctuation.

Skills:

Varying vocabulary   Stylistics
Adding depth by using models   Narrative structures
Technical accuracy
Sentence types and openers
Genre conventions

Year 9 – Masters of English creative writing

Skills:

Varying vocabulary
Adding depth by using models
Technical accuracy
Sentence types and openers
Genre conventions

Year 8 – Extended story writing

Skills:

Varying vocabulary
Adding depth by using models
Technical accuracy

Year 7 – Horror creative writing

Figure 3.1. A ladder showing the progression of a unit between Year 7 and 11 in English

Importantly, there need to be opportunities for the new teacher to contribute and create schemes for the curriculum and to learn from more experienced colleagues as they do so. The skills and expertise of colleagues in curriculum design will be vital to an early career teacher, as they have not yet accumulated the knowledge about what possible misconceptions may be likely or how they might best help students to master important concepts. If possible misconceptions are discussed, then hinge questions can be planned carefully together to really help gauge individual students' understanding. This is why it is key that the whole department takes collective responsibility for the development of the NQT, not just the mentor. Hattie (2012) discusses how beneficial it is for new teachers to work with and learn from others. It is essential that your mentee can take advantage of the knowledge, experience and expertise around them in their departments, across the school and even in other schools. Hattie (2012: 37) encourages teachers to work together so they can 'develop plans, develop common understandings on what is worth teaching, collaborate on understanding their beliefs of challenge and progress and work together to evaluate the impact of their planning on student outcomes'. This support and scaffolding will then help to develop an early career teacher's skills and confidence, so they are able to successfully plan their own lessons and resources.

Furthermore, as new teachers are still learning to balance their workload, observing how experienced teachers go about carrying out curriculum planning in a timely way is also helpful. Dylan Wiliam and Siobhán Leahy (2017: 9) observe that 'novice teachers typically take around four hours to prepare one hour of instruction, while expert teachers plan lessons of higher quality in five minutes or less. In other words, planning a lesson is something an expert does as much as fifty times faster than a novice. The more often we do things, the better and faster we get.' After a collaborative planning session, it would be prudent to spend some time in your meetings identifying what it is that more experienced colleagues do that enables them to do this. What are the processes and stages, and how can they be adapted when the NQT is working in a more solo capacity?

Evidently, subject knowledge is also hugely important when delivering a high standard of teaching. New entrants to the profession have joined at an interesting and fascinating time: many education publishers are releasing books on wider school issues, but many are also producing books which aim to enhance teachers' subject knowledge and offer insights into the way they teach their subject. As an English specialist, books such as Jennifer Webb's *How to Teach English Literature: Overcoming Cultural Poverty* (2019) have been instrumental in developing my own practice and making me reflect on what I could do differently. To find out what subject knowledge books have been important to teachers in other subject disciplines, I took to Twitter and asked teachers for their recommendations – a list of these is provided at the end of this chapter.

The good thing is that teachers are usually great at reflecting on their own weaknesses and gaps in knowledge. My own English degree contained little Shakespeare, so when I became a teacher in my late twenties, I had somehow never read *Macbeth* or even heard of *Mice and Men*! I knew that I needed to develop my knowledge in these areas before I even attempted to teach students these texts. A few years ago, I decided to swap *Macbeth* for *Julius Caesar* with a high ability group I was teaching, and I spent the entire summer reading the play and highlighting and annotating it myself, while researching the context and reading articles from the British Library. Becoming a student myself for a while ensured that I felt prepared and confident when the new term started.

The concept of teachers becoming students again is a great way to look at developing subject knowledge. Providing your mentee with an academic journal once every half term on a topic they teach, which you can then discuss together and create resources from, can be a really joyful experience for both the new teacher and yourself. We can sometimes get stuck in a rut with the things we are teaching, so refreshing our own knowledge can reignite our passion for our subject. However, do try to provide your NQT with the topics they will be teaching in good time so that they have the opportunity to do this. Completing a RAG (red, amber, green) writing subject audit with your NQT may also help them focus on their strengths and weaknesses and guide their own development.

Table 3.1. English subject knowledge audit example – *Macbeth*

Key concepts for teaching	How confident am I? (red – not confident at all, amber – need more revision/research, green – confident)
Contextual information on Shakespeare – his motivations and political ideology (beliefs).	
Contextual information on Jacobean society when the play was first performed (1606) and King James' beliefs (e.g. witches, Gunpowder Plot, divine right of kings).	
The relevance of stage directions throughout the play.	
The structure of the play: • The significance of the three visits to the witches. • Cyclical structure of the play – starts and ends with a traitor being beheaded. Hidden message about plotting to kill a king?	
The depiction of Macbeth throughout the play: • Character/relationships/fatal flaw/Aristotle's tragic hero/how he changes throughout the play.	
The depiction of Lady Macbeth throughout the play: • Character/relationships/flaws/challenges convention in patriarchal society/how she changes throughout the play.	
The depiction of Banquo throughout the play: • Character/relationships/flaws/attitudes to witches/foil to Macbeth's tragic hero/how he changes throughout the play.	

Key concepts for teaching	How confident am I? (red – not confident at all, amber – need more revision/research, green – confident)
The depiction of Macduff throughout the play: • Character/relationships/flaws/attitudes to Macbeth/ how he changes throughout the play.	
The depiction of the witches throughout the play: • Character/language they use/pathetic fallacy/trochaic tetrameter/how they change Macbeth throughout the play/relevance to King James/holy trinity subverting religion.	
The character of King Duncan: • What we learn about him as a ruler. • How Shakespeare uses him to show what great kingship is. • King Duncan as a foil to Macbeth.	
The theme of fate and free will: • How Shakespeare uses the witches to make Macbeth break the Great Chain of Being and subvert the divine right of kings. • How Shakespeare uses the fate of Macbeth and those who try to influence fate as a mouthpiece for his criticisms of those who are trying to overthrow King James. • How Banquo allows his fate to happen, unlike Macbeth.	
The theme of ambition and power: • How the different characters present their ambition, particularly Lady Macbeth.	

Key concepts for teaching	How confident am I? (red – not confident at all, amber – need more revision/research, green – confident)
• Concepts of masculinity and ambition. • What is Shakespeare's message about ambition?	
The theme of the supernatural: • The context of the Jacobean era and King James' beliefs. • The three scenes with the witches and how they are presented. • Subversion of religion and mentions of the devil. • Banquo's ghost as a manifestation of guilt. • Hallucinations of blood as a recurring motif and an extended metaphor for guilt.	

Ensure that you encourage the new teacher to spend some of their extra non-contact time on observing colleagues in other departments and in other schools/settings. It is tempting to use PPA for admin or marking, but observing other colleagues will really help to develop a new teacher's pedagogy much more than admin tasks. Additionally, as students can sometimes find it difficult to transfer knowledge from one discipline to the next, it would be useful to see how teachers in other lessons are teaching similar skills or content. An example of this might be a PE teacher observing a biology lesson or a drama teacher watching an English lesson in which they are studying a play they have been acting out in their drama lessons. In your discussions with your mentee, you could reflect on domain-specific knowledge they have witnessed, but also on how students could apply the skills and knowledge they were taught in that lesson across the curriculum.

I heard Alex Quigley speak at a researchED National Conference a few years ago. He recalled an experience where he had followed a student around school for the day and was struck by the way that they almost had to become a vocabulary tourist who needed to understand the domain-specific vocabulary in each subject and also the nuances between the variation in meaning of the same words in certain subjects –

particularly in relation to marking schemes and skills descriptors. An example of this is the word 'evaluate': in English lessons, it might mean to judge the significance of a piece of evidence or a statement; whereas in maths, it means to substitute a number for each variable and perform the arithmetic operations. Remembering all of these nuances and subject-specific definitions is a difficult feat, so it is no wonder that students sometimes struggle to organise their knowledge into more complex mental models. Encourage the new teacher to explore the tier 3 vocabulary and tier 2 command words that are important in their subject and ask them to define them. They could then work with other NQTs in the school or the literacy coordinator to spot where there are crossovers in other subject areas, or where the same command words mean different things in different subjects. This will give your mentee a whole school project to really challenge them; they could later present their findings to the department.

Rosenshine's principles (discussed in the research section earlier in this chapter) are an excellent baseline to guide your mentee on how to structure the content of their lessons. Tom Sherrington (2018) has provided a useful lesson planning tool on his blog which is based on the ten principles. This could be used once a week to help the new teacher plan retrieval and spaced practice activities, while also developing their resource bank of analogies and exemplars to scaffold and deepen students' learning. It isn't meant to be an onerous task but is more of a checklist for planning. It would work particularly well when planning for the medium term as well as for lessons, as it highlights where the big ideas and concepts come in a learning journey. It could also be used as a reflection tool after lessons or completed while observing others. Any boxes that are not filled in or are unclear should offer really specific feedback about how they can improve or develop the lesson plan for next time.

It is important that lessons begin with a recall of previous learning, so your mentee should be encouraged to explore various ways of doing this to help build and strengthen the knowledge schema in students' minds. They should also be given the opportunity to practise live modelling with a visualiser or on the whiteboard – as, unlike pre-prepared model answers, this demonstrates how the information should be analysed, evaluated and presented. In this way, the students will be much more confident when doing it themselves as they get to witness the journey to the correct answer in real time and can break it down into steps they can easily follow. Modelling live can be nerve-wracking at first, as teachers often feel that they should appear to know all the answers. However, you can help to ease the stress by preparing ideas in advance or taking a look at a department bank of responses for guidance. It is good to involve the students in the drafting process too, by asking them questions such as 'What do you think comes next?' or 'What should I write or include here?' You could demonstrate this to your mentee during a lesson observation or you could team teach some modelling with one of the NQT's classes. In the same way that we have high expectations of the students, and they often rise to the challenge, early career teachers will too – with guidance and scaffolds that can be taken away gradually.

When it comes to resources for lessons, there is a huge community of teachers on EduTwitter who freely and generously share their wisdom, expertise and resources for free. Twitter is also a superb way to become involved in professional conversations with colleagues from across the world. You could encourage your new colleague to join Twitter – even if they want to do it incognito or not post themselves. It is an amazing world of debate and information that is easy to get sucked into, but there is also incredible knowledge and ideas which are great for stimulating thinking and creativity.

Finally, as has been stressed in this chapter and the related standard, the importance of literacy in every subject area cannot be underestimated. It is every teacher's responsibility to develop students' literacy by modelling high quality oral language, promoting reading for pleasure and teaching different forms of writing. It is essential that you encourage your mentee to read the EEF's *Improving Literacy* guidance reports (2016b, 2017, 2019) and their seven recommendations in the 2019 guidance. Ask the NQT to identify where the recommendations are present in pre-existing medium-term plans and to come up with some ideas for how to incorporate other opportunities to promote literacy. If your school is lucky enough to have a library, your mentee could collaborate with the librarian to plan events or extra-curricular clubs to improve students' literacy and raise its profile across the school, which will also give them some experience of organising a whole school event.

Further reading – developing subject knowledge

These are only a small selection of the books available but were highlighted on Twitter by experienced teachers as being those that had most developed their own subject knowledge.

Primary

Bowden, A. and Cross, A. (2014) *Essential Primary Science*. Maidenhead: Open University Press.

Cope, A. and Spendlow, S. (2015) *The Art of Being a Brilliant Primary Teacher*. Carmarthen: Crown House Publishing.

Crystal, D. (2004) *Rediscover Grammar*, 3rd edn. London: Longman.

Gamble, N. (2013) *Exploring Children's Literature: Reading with Pleasure and Purpose*. Newbury Park: Sage.

Haylock, D. and Manning, R. (2018) *Mathematics Explained for Primary Teachers*. London: SAGE.

Payne, J. and Scott, M. (2017) *Making Every Primary Lesson Count: Six Principles to Support Great Teaching and Learning*. Carmarthen: Crown House Publishing.

Tennent, W., Reedy, D., Hobsbaum, A. and Gamble, N. (2016) *Guiding Readers – Layers of Meaning: A Handbook for Teaching Reading Comprehension to 7–11 Year Olds*. London: UCL Institute of Education Press.

Secondary

Art and design

Addison, N. (2014) *Learning to Teach Art and Design in the Secondary School*. Abingdon and New York: Routledge.

Beloeil, G. and Riabovitchev, D. (2013) *Art Fundamentals: Color, Light, Composition, Anatomy, Perspective, and Depth*. Worcester: 3dtotal Publishing.

Briggs, P. (2016) *Make, Build, Create: Sculpture Products for Children*. London: Black Dog Publishing.

Hickman, R. (2004) *Art Education 11–18*. London: Continuum.

Business studies

Jephcote, M. and Abbott, I. (2006) *Teaching Business Education 14–19*. Abingdon and New York: Routledge.

Computer studies/ICT

Lau, W. (2017) *Teaching Computing in Secondary Schools*. Abingdon and New York: Routledge.

Simmons, C. and Hawkins, C. (2015) *Teaching Computing* (Developing as a Reflective Secondary Teacher). London: SAGE.

Design technology

Owen-Jackson, G. (2013) *Debates in Design and Technology Education*. Abingdon and New York: Routledge.

Owen-Jackson, G. (2015) *Learning to Teach Design and Technology in the Secondary School*. Abingdon and New York: Routledge.

Spendlove, D. (2008) *100 Ideas for Teaching Design and Technology*. London: Continuum.

Drama

Fleming, M. (2017) *Starting Drama Teaching*. Abingdon and New York: Routledge.

English

Beadle, P. (2015) *How to Teach Literacy*. Carmarthen: Independent Thinking Press.

Curtis, C. (2019) *How to Teach English: Novels, Non-Fiction and Their Artful Navigation*. Carmarthen: Independent Thinking Press.

Lemov, D., Driggs, C. and Woolway, E. (2016) *Reading Reconsidered: A Practical Guide to Rigorous Literacy Instruction*. San Francisco, CA: Jossey-Bass.

Pryke, S. and Stanithorpe, A. (2020) *Ready to Teach Macbeth: The What, the How and Why for English Teachers*. Woodbridge: John Catt Educational.

Quigley, A. (2018) *Closing the Vocabulary Gap*. London: David Fulton.

Roberts, M. (2020) *You Can't Revise for GCSE English! Yes You Can, and Mark Roberts Shows You How*. New York: Collins.

Tharby, A. (2017) *Making Every English Lesson Count: Six Principles to Support Great Reading and Writing*. Carmarthen: Crown House Publishing.

Webb, J. (2019) *How to Teach English Literature: Overcoming Cultural Poverty*. Woodbridge: John Catt Educational.

Webb, J. (2020) *Teach Like a Writer: Expert Tips on Teaching Students to Write in Different Forms*. Woodbridge: John Catt Educational.

Geography

Biddulph, M. (2015) *Learning to Teach Geography in the Secondary School*. Abingdon and New York: Routledge.

Enser, M. (2019) *Making Every Geography Lesson Count: Six Principles to Support Great Geography Teaching*. Carmarthen: Crown House Publishing.

History

Morris, M. (2013) *The Norman Conquest*. London: Windmill Books.

Runeckles, C. (2018) *Making Every History Lesson Count: Six Principles to Support Great History Teaching*. Carmarthen: Crown House Publishing.

Thorne, S. (2018) *Becoming an Outstanding History Teacher*. Abingdon and New York: Routledge.

Maths

Barton, C. (2018) *How I Wish I'd Taught Maths: Lessons Learned from Research, Conversations with Experts, and 12 Years of Mistakes*. Woodbridge: John Catt Educational.

Boaler, J. (2015) *The Elephant in the Classroom: Helping Children Learn and Love Maths*. London: Souvenir Press.

Chambers, P. and Timlin, R. (2013) *Teaching Mathematics in the Secondary School*. London: SAGE.

Gates, P. (2001) *Issues in Mathematics Teaching*. Abingdon and New York: Routledge.

McCrea, E. (2019) *Making Every Maths Lesson Count: Six Principles to Support Great Maths Teaching*. Carmarthen: Crown House Publishing.

Mattock, P. (2019) *Visible Maths: Using Representations and Structure to Enhance Mathematics Teaching in Schools*. Carmarthen: Crown House Publishing.

Morgan, J. (2019) *A Compendium of Mathematical Methods: A Handbook for School Teachers*. Woodbridge: John Catt Educational.

Ollerton, M. and Sykes, P. (2006) *Getting the Buggers to Add Up*. London: Continuum.

Southall, E. (2017) *Yes But Why? Teaching for Understanding in Mathematics*. London: SAGE.

Watson, A., Jones, K. and Pratt, D. (2013) *Key Ideas in Teaching Mathematics: Research-Based Guidance for Ages 9–19*. Oxford: Oxford University Press.

Media studies

Dixon, M. (2019) *Media Theory for A Level: The Essential Revision Guide*. Abingdon and New York: Routledge.

Laughey, D. (2009) *Media Studies: Theories and Approaches*. Harpenden: Kamera Books.

Modern foreign languages

Conti, G. and Smit, S. (2019) *Breaking the Sound Barrier: Teaching Language Learners How to Listen*. Self-published.

Driscoll, P. (2013) *Debates in Modern Languages Education*. Abingdon and New York: Routledge.

Hazell, C. (2020) *Independent Thinking on MFL: How to Make Modern Foreign Language Teaching Exciting, Inclusive and Relevant*. Carmarthen: Independent Thinking Press.

Maxwell, J. (2019) *Making Every MFL Lesson Count: Six Principles to Support Modern Foreign Language Teaching*. Carmarthen: Crown House Publishing.

Pachler, N. (2013) *Learning to Teach Foreign Languages in the Secondary School*. Abingdon and New York: Routledge.

Music

Cooke, C. (2016) *Learning to Teach Music in the Secondary School*. Abingdon and New York: Routledge.

Jackson, N. (2009) *The Little Book of Music for the Classroom: Using Music to Improve Memory, Motivation, Learning and Creativity*. Carmarthen: Crown House Publishing.

PE

Capel, S. (2012) *Debates in Physical Education*. Abingdon and New York: Routledge.

Stidder, G. and Hayes, S. (2016) *The Really Useful Physical Education Book*. Abingdon and New York: Routledge.

Personal, social, health and economic education

Rae, T. and Black, P. (2011) *The Emotional Curriculum for Young Adults KS4*. Abingdon and New York: Routledge.

Religious studies

Lewis, A. and Orme, R. (2017) *World Religions: Judaism, Christianity and Islam* (KS3 Knowing Religion). Glasgow: Collins.

McGrath, A. E. (2016) *Christian Theology: An Introduction*. Chichester: Wiley-Blackwell.

Science

Allison, S. (2017) *Making Every Science Lesson Count: Six Principles to Support Great Science Teaching*. Carmarthen: Crown House Publishing.

Green, C. (2016) *How to Teach Secondary Science*. Carmarthen: Independent Thinking Press.

Taber, K. (2002) *Chemical Misconceptions: Prevention, Diagnosis and Care*. Vol. I: *Theoretical Background*. London: Royal Society of Chemistry.

Chapter 3: Summary

Identify goal:
To demonstrate good subject knowledge by delivering a carefully sequenced and coherent curriculum, which supports students to build complex mental models, develop fluency and improve students' literacy.

Standard 3 – Demonstrate good subject and curriculum knowledge

Evaluate and reflect on the standard:
- Are there still areas of subject knowledge that the NQT needs to develop? What useful strategies have they picked up from other, more experienced colleagues to help them plan sequences of lessons?
- Ask them to rate their confidence and identify areas where they need more support.
- Create an action plan for further reading and next steps to develop their skills.

Apply the learning:
- Ask them to complete a RAG rating of subject knowledge for each unit to be taught, and read some books/journal articles to improve in that area. Produce some resources for the rest of the department to use which demonstrate the new knowledge and strategies.
- After reading Rosenshine's principles, advise the NQT to spend time using the planning tool from Tom Sherrington's (2018) blog post to plan lessons and reflect on lessons that have been delivered. Then they can use the tool to observe others, so that meaningful, targeted feedback can be given.
- Encourage them to join Twitter and find some resources that could be used in one of the schemes. Bring them to the meeting and create a home learning booklet for use with a unit.

Come up with a plan:

- Together come up with a list of what a coherent and well-sequenced curriculum looks like and discuss.
- Together use your department's curriculum map to plot out using a ladder diagram how the skills build on one another vertically. How could they be improved/developed?
- Encourage the NQT to explore the national curriculum and key skills that students need to learn. How do they fit into your department's curriculum map?
- Schedule time to plan collaboratively with more experienced colleagues.
- Schedule lesson observations within and outside of the department, and in other schools, with a focus on how analogies, demonstrations and examples are used by teachers.

Learn together:

- Both read John Hattie's *Visible Learning* (2012), particularly part 2 on lessons. Discuss the findings and how you can both integrate them into your own practice.
- Use the seven recommendations in the EEF's *Improving Literacy in Secondary Schools* (2019) guidance report to collaboratively plan activities and resources for lessons.
- Spend time together compiling and defining the tier 2 and 3 vocabulary in your subject discipline and cross-reference these with other departments.
- Each half term, provide your NQT with an academic journal about a topic you teach. After you have both read it, discuss the articles and produce some resources for the department.

Chapter 4

Plan and teach well-structured lessons

Classroom practice (Standard 4 – Plan and teach well-structured lessons)	
Learn that ...	**Learn how to ...**
1. Effective teaching can transform pupils' knowledge, capabilities and beliefs about learning. 2. Effective teachers introduce new material in steps, explicitly linking new ideas to what has been previously studied and learned. 3. Modelling helps pupils understand new processes and ideas; good models make abstract ideas concrete and accessible. 4. Guides, scaffolds and worked examples can help pupils apply new ideas, but should be gradually removed as pupil expertise increases.	**Plan effective lessons, by:** • *Using modelling, explanations and scaffolds, acknowledging that novices need more structure early in a domain.* • *Enabling critical thinking and problem-solving by first teaching the necessary foundational content knowledge.* • *Removing scaffolding only when pupils are achieving a high degree of success in applying previously taught material.* • *Providing sufficient opportunity for pupils to consolidate and practise applying new knowledge and skills.*

Classroom practice (Standard 4 – Plan and teach well-structured lessons)

Learn that …	Learn how to …
5. Explicitly teaching pupils metacognitive strategies linked to subject knowledge, including how to plan, monitor and evaluate, supports independence and academic success.	• *Breaking tasks down into constituent components when first setting up independent practice (e.g. using tasks that scaffold pupils through metacognitive and procedural processes).*
6. Questioning is an essential tool for teachers; questions can be used for many purposes, including to check pupils' prior knowledge, assess understanding and break down problems.	**Make good use of expositions, by:** • *Starting expositions at the point of current pupil understanding.* • *Combining a verbal explanation with a relevant graphical representation of the same concept or process, where appropriate.*
7. High quality classroom talk can support pupils to articulate key ideas, consolidate understanding and extend their vocabulary.	• *Using concrete representation of abstract ideas (e.g. making use of analogies, metaphors, examples and non-examples).*
8. Practice is an integral part of effective teaching; ensuring pupils have repeated opportunities to practise, with appropriate guidance and support, increases success.	**Model effectively, by:** • *Narrating thought processes when modelling to make explicit how experts think (e.g. asking questions aloud that pupils should consider when working independently and drawing pupils' attention to links with prior knowledge).*
9. Paired and group activities can increase pupil success, but to work together effectively pupils need guidance, support and practice.	• *Making the steps in a process memorable and ensuring pupils can recall them (e.g. naming them, developing mnemonics or linking to memorable stories).*
10. How pupils are grouped is also important; care should be taken to monitor the impact of groupings on pupil attainment, behaviour and motivation.	• *Exposing potential pitfalls and explaining how to avoid them.*

Classroom practice (Standard 4 – Plan and teach well-structured lessons)	
Learn that …	**Learn how to …**
11. Homework can improve pupil outcomes, particularly for older pupils, but it is likely that the quality of homework and its relevance to main class teaching is more important than the amount set.	**Stimulate pupil thinking and check for understanding, by:** • *Planning activities around what you want pupils to think hard about.* • *Including a range of types of questions in class discussions to extend and challenge pupils (e.g. by modelling new vocabulary or asking pupils to justify answers).* • *Providing appropriate wait time between question and response where more developed responses are required.* • *Considering the factors that will support effective collaborative or paired work (e.g. familiarity with routines, whether pupils have the necessary prior knowledge and how pupils are grouped).* • *Providing scaffolds for pupil talk to increase the focus and rigour of dialogue.*

Notes

Learn that … statements are informed by the best available educational research.

Learn how to … statements are drawn from a wider evidence base including both academic research and additional guidance from expert practitioners.

Why is this standard important? What does the research say?

Sequencing

Great teachers design lesson activities, resources, assessments and feedback to max-imise the opportunity for each of their students to understand concepts, develop skills and deepen their knowledge whilst also fuelling their motivation and seeking to support their broader development as well-rounded individuals. (Sherrington, 2017a: 38)

This quote from *The Learning Rainforest* sums up for me what great educators do: they transform students' knowledge and beliefs about the validity of studying by developing their learning and making them feel confident about their own capabili-ties. As discussed in previous chapters, some of this comes from not overloading students with new information and instead introducing unfamiliar material in steps, so they are able to see how the fresh ideas link explicitly to what has previously been studied. Chunking information or tasks is important, as it allows us to take smaller bits of information and combine them into more meaningful wholes, or as neuroscientist Daniel Bor (2012) calls it, 'hacking' the limits of our memory. He suggests that, as learners, we have a natural tendency to make connections and see patterns, and chunking allows us to do this much more easily than being flooded with information and feeling unable to make sense of it.

Bor believes it also inspires creativity, and the creator of Apple and Macintosh com-puters, the late Steve Jobs, agreed with him. When he was interviewed for *Wired* magazine in 1995, he said 'creativity is just connecting things … they were able to connect experiences they've had and synthesise new things' (Wolf, 1996). He was speaking about creating new products, but the same can be said for learning. Great learners think about what they have learned before and are able to make connections and even speculate about what might come next. It is our job as educators to facili-tate and foster that creativity by ensuring our planning and lessons are well sequenced and well structured.

Part of this sequencing needs to be based around the understanding that novices in a new topic need more structure early on in the learning domain. Research in the field of educational psychology shows that learning from examples and models, sometimes called example-based learning, is much more effective than learning through problem-solving, particularly in the early phases of cognitive skill acquisition (Atkinson et al., 2000; Renkl, 2005). Example-based learning is usually designed so that learners receive a general introduction where new concepts are introduced, which then leads on to worked examples which show these concepts and principles being used. The evidence suggests that it is best for learners if the solution steps are demonstrated live, so they can logically work their way through, knowing the cognitive steps they need to take to achieve the final goal (Wittwer and Renkl, 2010).

Models and example-based learning

The science behind the success of using models and example-based learning with novice learners can be traced back to cognitive load theory, which was explored in Chapter 2. As Sweller (Sweller et al., 1998; Sweller, 2005) discovered, when learners are exposed to an unfamiliar knowledge base, they have to search for solutions to a problem independently, which may put demands on the capacity of their working memory, as they do not have a deep understanding or the schemata to solve the problem. When they have a worked example, students do not need to search for irrelevant processes; instead, their cognitive resources are freed up to engage in actively understanding the solution procedure, with some help from their new subject knowledge. Their brains are free to connect the subject knowledge and construct problem-solving schemata that can then be used flexibly to acquire new knowledge later on and even applied to new situations when they are asked to problem-solve (Van Gog et al., 2004).

Additionally, the use of a good model makes abstract ideas more concrete and accessible, which is why it is so important that procedural skills are demonstrated, so learners do not produce faulty self-explanations and misconceptions can be eradicated. For example, in English, when you tell a student that they are required to evaluate, it is much clearer for them to be shown how to evaluate than just to be told that they need to demonstrate this skill. Furthermore, when instructional explanations are combined with worked examples, students are able to detect inconsistencies in their own learning, so they are not simply under the illusion that they understand how to do a task, which can inhibit learning later on when they come to the independent practising phase (Chi et al., 1994). This is why scaffolding is so crucial: it is another form of support that the teacher can offer to move the students towards a deeper understanding (Wood et al., 1976). Scaffolding should give students enough contingent support to tackle problems that are manageable, so that deep processing can take place. A study by Wertsch (1979) demonstrated that when students have contingent scaffolding support, they know which steps to take and are able to later proceed independently. When they don't, they withdraw from the task and may feel frustrated that it is either beyond their reach or they don't know how to proceed, and so become bored and exasperated. This is why scaffolds are so important.

Of course, as students develop more expertise, the scaffolds should be removed gradually, as frequent interruptions to learning or over-scaffolding may disrupt the learning process of students with more developed prior knowledge (Cohen, 1994). This can lead to the expertise reversal effect: more established expert learners may find the structured steps detrimental because processing redundant information can cause unnecessary working memory overload and distract them from the concepts that still need to be learned (Renkl and Atkinson, 2007). However, as Rosenshine (2012) states, scaffolds should only begin to be taken away when students are achieving a high degree of success in applying previously taught material – around 80%. This will give them the confidence to be able to independently plan and evaluate their own learning and therefore achieve academic success.

Metacognition

To help students manage their own learning, the evidence suggests that it is key to explicitly teach metacognitive strategies which are linked to subject knowledge. The EEF's guidance report *Metacognition and Self-Regulated Learning* (2018c) outlines seven key recommendations which offer a simplified framework for the implementation of self-regulated learning and metacognition strategies in the classroom. One of the first recommendations is that teachers need to explicitly teach students metacognitive strategies by ensuring that the concepts of plan, monitor and evaluate are specifically applied to content and tasks in subject areas. One way of doing this could be by using a series of steps which activate prior knowledge, which then lead to independent practice and a form of structured self-reflection. The report advocates a seven-step model for explicitly teaching these strategies and also offers a worked example of them in use in a history lesson. As the report states, metacognitive strategies are much stronger when they are specific to the subject and task, and they highlight the fact that it is 'very hard to have knowledge about how one can learn in a subject without solid subject knowledge' (EEF, 2018c: 15). Therefore, if you want students to improve through practice, they need to apply the skills to different tasks repeatedly.

Another important recommendation is that teachers should explicitly support students to develop independent learning skills through a mixture of guided practice (which will be removed gradually so they can develop the skills and strategies to apply them to independent practice) and timely effective feedback. What is more, Zimmerman (2002) suggests that if students are taught to truly self-regulate their learning, it can compensate for their individual differences in learning, meaning that barriers to learning can be alleviated through students' awareness of their own personal limitations and how they can compensate for these. He states: 'although teachers need to know student's limitations in learning, their goal should be to empower their students to become self-aware of these differences. If a student fails to understand some aspect of a lesson in class, he or she must possess the self-awareness and strategic knowledge to take corrective action' (Zimmerman, 2002: 65). This ability to self-regulate is also closely connected to motivation, as there will come a time when students will have to manage and balance their goals on their own, particularly when it comes to revision tasks. Teachers can help them to do this by following a number of evidence informed strategies, which will be outlined later in this chapter.

Questioning

Clearly, in order for students to successfully adopt metacognitive strategies, it is important that the teacher is able to ascertain what their current understanding is, so they are able to start expositions at an appropriate point. A great tool for assessing understanding is questioning, which can be used to check students' prior knowledge and break down any problems into steps so that they become more manageable. One of the questioning techniques that has been successful in studies is elaborative interrogation: prompting students to answer 'why' questions. Research shows that the key to using elaborative interrogation in the classroom is to explicitly state a fact and then prompt learners to generate an explanation for it (Dunlosky et al., 2013) – for example, asking 'Why would X fact be true and not some other?' It works well to enhance learning because learners 'activate schemata' and 'these schemata in turn, help to organize new information which facilitates new retrieval' (Willoughby and Wood, 1994: 140).

However, studies also reveal that students must be able to discriminate among related facts, and process both similarities and differences between related things, so that elaborations are precise and self-generated. Unlike scaffolds, which work well with novice learners, elaborative interrogation effects are larger when prior knowledge is higher rather than lower (Rawson and Van Overschelde, 2008), so they will really challenge students and move them on. In order to use questioning well, teachers need to stimulate student thinking and create a culture of enquiry in their classrooms and place questioning at the centre of their pedagogy. Planning activities around what they want students to think hard about is much simpler when lessons are planned around different types of questions, including hinge questions, which will be discussed later on in this chapter.

Oracy and dialogic teaching

Promoting high quality classroom talk and oracy is one way of ensuring that the answers to questions are well discussed and promote deeper learning. Dialogic teaching is an approach which aims to increase student engagement, learning and attainment, particularly from those who come from disadvantaged backgrounds (Alexander, 2003, 2005). Dialogic teaching promotes dialogue which encourages students to reason, discuss, argue and explain their thoughts and reasoning, thereby developing their higher-order thinking and improving articulacy. It is the opposite of monologic talk (Lyle, 2008), which is usually dominated by the teacher and includes students mostly as part of an initiation–response feedback pattern, where a teacher asks a question and then waits for a student response by putting up their hands. Instead, a dialogic approach utilises the 'building blocks of dialogue' (Jay et al., 2017: 10) as the questions are structured to prompt more questions and the talk is more cumulative (Alexander, 2008).

In an efficacy trial in 2015–2016 (Jay et al., 2017), 38 primary schools which used dialogic teaching intervention methods were measured against 38 control schools which carried on with 'business as usual'. The children in the dialogic teaching schools made two additional months of progress in English and science and one month of additional progress in maths, compared to children in the control schools, on average, while those on free school meals made two months of extra progress in English, science and maths, compared to their peers in the control schools. In addition, the teachers involved in the study spoke about how they had reflected on their pedagogy and now felt able to use questioning more skilfully, with them no longer relying on using a series of unconnected questions but instead having follow-up questions in mind and then even further follow-up questions to develop the children's verbal reasoning. The teachers involved also discussed how it had improved their use of wait time when questioning, and observed that the quality and amount of student talk in their classrooms was sustained for longer. Like any new strategy, dialogic teaching needs to be employed over time and students will improve and develop with practice.

Practice makes perfect

Another ingredient of a well-structured, high quality lesson is the opportunity for students to practise using their new knowledge and skills repeatedly, with appropriate guidance and support from the teacher, so they are able to experience some successes. Practice testing does not just mean getting students to repeatedly complete exam questions or mock exams; it can include any low-stakes or no-stakes practice or any independent activity completed in class which is not a summative assessment. These can take the form of multiple-choice questions, gap-fill, practice problems or questions at the end of a chapter, as well as other exercises that students can engage in on their own.

Studies have shown that practice testing enhances learning and retention by producing two different kinds of testing effects: direct effects and mediated effects (Roediger and Karpicke, 2006). The direct effects change the learning because of the act of taking the test, because when students attempt to retrieve target information, they trigger an elaborate retrieval process by searching their long-term memory and activating related information, which then forms an elaborated trace with multiple pathways which students can use later to access that information (Carpenter, 2009). In contrast, the mediated effects change the learning that arises from the kind of encoding that takes place after the test – for example, in a later testing opportunity. Here, the encoding of more effective mediators, such as connecting cues and targets, is facilitated through the practice testing, supporting better retention and test performance (Pyc and Rawson, 2009).

It is important that students are given the opportunity to practise independently frequently, as final test performance is usually better when participants have had multiple practice tests rather than a single opportunity (Pavlik and Anderson, 2005). However, if the tests are conducted in immediate succession in a session, there are minimal effects compared to when testing is spaced (Cull, 2000). Furthermore, it seems that when it comes to the intervals between testing, longer is better (Carpenter et al., 2008). Distributed practice, where information is encountered on more than one occasion, can also help with this because learning over time benefits long-term retention more than cramming before a test in relatively rapid succession (Dunlosky et al., 2013). When we tell students to reread their notes or retrieve something from very recent memory, there is deficient processing as it is so close to the original learning episode. This can trick students into thinking that they have more secure knowledge of the subject content than they really do (Bahrick and Hall, 2005). Therefore, reviewing content by completing practice tests of things that were taught in a previous unit, during a different topic, may encourage students to develop their retrieval skills in a more meaningful way.

Collaborative learning approaches

Aside from practice testing, there are other strategies that the evidence highlights as being factors in increasing student success, such as group or collaborative work. Collaborative learning approaches involve students working together on group activities where they have been set a clearly assigned task in which everybody can participate. Research shows that the impact of group work and collaborative learning approaches is mostly positive, and that more structured approaches which promote interaction between group members and include well-designed tasks lead to the greatest progress and gains (EEF, 2018g). Interestingly, Kirschner at al. (2018) propose that when designing opportunities for collaborative learning, teachers should consider cognitive load, as this also influences the efficiency and effectiveness of collaborative learning. They state that there are certain principles at play in the way that biologically secondary knowledge is processed that specifically relate to group work. The borrowing and reorganising principle, for example, suggests that much of the information stored in our long-term memory has been borrowed from the long-term memories of others. This is then reorganised when we use information we have previously stored in our own long-term memories (Bartlett, 1932). Therefore, during collaboration, we can easily obtain some important information from other people which may be more difficult for us to acquire by other means of learning.

Kirschner et al. (2018) also describe the randomness of genesis principle: when we first generate information, if we are unable to obtain the evidence we need from others, we have to use our own primary skills to problem-solve by generating it ourselves. Problem-solving is only useful when we have no alternative access to solutions to problems; collaborative learning can provide this access by increasing the range of information and answers available to us. When grouping students, however, care should be taken to monitor the impact of groupings on motivation, behaviour and, ultimately, attainment. The EEF have published useful guidance in their 'Collaborative learning: Teaching and Learning Toolkit' (2018g); more specific advice on this can be found in the 'How can I help my mentee meet this standard?' section of this chapter.

Home learning

Finally, part of a teacher's planning is about providing opportunities for students to partake in quality homework or home learning. According to the EEF (2020), the impact of setting high quality homework is, on average, five months of additional progress, yet they also add the caveat that how the homework is set can have a huge effect on its impact. They suggest that homework is most effective when it is utilised as a short, concentrated intervention – for example, work which focuses on the improvement of a specific target, or a more routine task such as learning vocabulary or practice maths tests. However, homework has always been a contentious issue, particularly when John Hattie published his *Visible Learning* meta-analysis in 2009 and revealed that it had no effect on pupil achievement for primary school pupils. In 2014, Hattie was interviewed on BBC Radio 4 and said:

Homework in primary school has an effect of around zero. In high school it's larger ... which is why we need to get it right, not why we need to get rid of it. Five to ten minutes has the same effect of one hour to two hours. The worst thing you can do with homework is give kids projects. The best thing you can do is to reinforce some-thing you have already learned. (Montague, 2014)

The research shows that, if homework is set and done well, the effect size on second-ary school students has an average impact of 0.40. It can make a real difference if the right work is set, under the right conditions and it is not just seen as an add-on. To be successful, it needs to relate to the learning that students are doing in school and they need to be given quality feedback on the work they hand in.

In addition, MacBeath and Turner (1990) suggest that homework should be varied and manageable, with an element of challenge, but should not be too difficult to complete. If the correct balance is achieved, then homework should promote self-confidence and understanding and also give students the opportunity to use their own initiative and creativity. Many schools have embraced the idea of giving students more choice in the types of activities they complete for home learning by producing 'takeaway' style menus with varying levels of challenge. Russel Tarr (2015) suggests that this is a good idea because it is 'giving students the flexibility to choose the content and/or the outcome of their homework assignments ... which increases engagement and promotes independent learning'. What much of the research avail-able does have in common, though, is an agreement that the homework set needs to promote a greater love of learning and that the purpose of completing it should be clear to both students and parents. This will consequently result in them realising how important homework can be in moving on their learning and may result in them making more of an effort with it.

Focus group findings

Due to the workload and lack of time that some mentors had, a few participants in the focus group felt that their mentors hadn't spent enough time with them on exploring what makes a well-structured lesson. One participant spoke of how their mentor seemed to brush them off by acknowledging that they had a very different teaching style, so had already mastered their teaching environment. This was quite frustrating as the targets they were then given to develop their pedagogy were very vague and general. However, some were supported to improve specific areas of their pedagogy, such as questioning, and, after seeing other staff use them during lessons, were encouraged to trial school-wide approaches such as cold-call questioning.

Although some of the teachers questioned had been encouraged to look at how lessons were structured and sequenced during observations, many felt that their mentors probably thought that this was something foundational and basic which they would have been taught on their university/training courses, and therefore that this was already cemented when they started their NQT year. For some this came as a welcome assumption, as they already felt overwhelmed with work and didn't feel as if they had the capacity to explore different lesson structures on top of an increasing workload. But others felt frustrated by the lack of clarity on the best structure for a lesson, with one teacher revealing that 'a structure to follow and the rationale behind those steps would have made life a lot easier and made planning a lot quicker'. Some who were asked to use a specific structure and were told to stick to it were not given the rationale behind it, so instead of seeing it as something important, they almost saw it as a prison they were trapped within and didn't really understand why.

Some early career teachers in the study felt that the amount of planning they were expected to do, and the amount of related paperwork they had to complete, was not conducive to a positive work–life balance, with one teacher recounting that they spent most evenings and weekends working and filling in detailed pro formas which seemed extraneous when it came to actually teaching the lesson. The same teacher felt that instead their mentor should have spent time showing them different ways of assessing gaps in student knowledge and how to translate that into more fluid planning, which would help them to pitch their lessons and expositions more appropriately. Some mentors did recognise that their mentees were struggling with planning and workload and offered to help, but one recalled an occasion when they had asked for some help and had been told that this is just what primary teaching is like and if they couldn't hack it now, they would be better off finding something else to do and not wasting their time. Fortunately, instances like this were few and far between in the interviews I conducted, and although early career teachers acknowledged that the planning and workload was tough, they mostly felt that they had been supported as much as they could be.

Another teacher spoke about the frustration they felt when they were trying to devise learning outcomes/objectives for their lessons, as they were spending a lot of valuable planning time formulating and rewriting the aims of the lesson. Their mentor gave them some valuable advice – to think about what they wanted the learners to be able to do after the lesson – and this simplified things. The straightforward and practical nature of the guidance was appreciated: 'The best advice and help I received when looking at the content of lessons were things that I could easily grasp and apply to my own classroom. I often didn't have the headspace to work with woolly definitions and ideas.'

Nearly all of the participants had received training on metacognition and understood what the general principles were, but fewer felt that they had a deep enough understanding of the principles to be able to use it properly in their lessons. Some had asked about it and felt that their mentors also didn't really know what it meant!

They were more clear about how important literacy and oracy were to learning, and many had been involved in creating resources for the department to use in lessons and had attended CPD sessions on how to do this.

How can I help my mentee meet this standard?

When assisting your mentee with their planning and teaching, you cannot take for granted that they are familiar with the best ways of teaching well-structured lessons, as evidenced by the educational research. Different training providers have their own ideologies and ideas about what constitutes a 'good' lesson, and while these are all extremely valid, for the purpose of this book we are following the Early Career Framework's lead in looking towards research on cognitive science, and the way students learn, to reveal best practice. In previous standards, it has been recommended that your mentee reads about Rosenshine's principles for some insights into the structure of lessons and how they can be used to introduce new information in steps, taking account of prior learning and avoiding cognitive overload. It is worth revisiting his research on modelling and scaffolds here as they are so crucial in giving novice learners the structure they need early in the domain.

The fourth of his ten principles of instruction advises teachers to 'Provide models: Providing students with models and worked examples can help them learn to solve problems faster' (Rosenshine, 2012: 15). During your meetings, it would be worth discussing the kinds of modelling that can be employed in lessons and looking at examples. The power of a worked example, where teachers provide 'a step-by-step demonstration of how to perform a task or how to solve a problem' (Rosenshine, 2012: 15) cannot be underestimated, therefore it would be useful to help organise some observations of staff across different subject areas who regularly use worked examples as part of their practice. Rosenshine states that 'master teachers' often 'provide students with many worked examples so that the general patterns are clear, providing a strong basis from which to learn', whereas less effective teachers do not 'provide enough worked examples' (Sherrington, 2019: 21). This can lead to cognitive overload and students being unsure of how to apply the new procedures they have been taught.

Your mentee may not find this process as simple as it sounds. It takes a level of confidence and security in subject knowledge to be able to share cognitive thought processes aloud, particularly to older children. It can also be difficult to strike the right balance between guiding and supporting and giving the answers, as, ideally, after giving students worked examples, they should be able to finish problems more independently. This is why the learning steps in the worked examples need to be clear because they will be expected to complete these processes themselves later on. Both Rosenshine and Sherrington believe that using many worked examples supports students' development of mastery, which is when scaffolding and other instructional supports can be gradually withdrawn.

Some fantastic teachers on Twitter gave me their tips for modelling and using worked examples, which may be useful to pass on as ideas to your NQT. @missfordenglish spoke about how she keeps her own exercise book in which she completes all of her models and then shares them via the visualiser (see Figure 4.1). Not only can she then refer back to them in future lessons, but if a student has been absent she can photocopy the model for them from her book. Another teacher, @noncontacttime, said that they record complex processes and put them on a shared drive for students to use. They model the task and then point the students to the videos if they are unsure. After about five minutes, they then ask a student to model the task again.

During some of your meeting times, ask the mentee to bring something they can model to you while you film. You can then watch it back and write down the processes they took to get to the finished work. These written instructions should be the kind of dialogue that teachers demonstrate to students when they are completing worked examples. In this vein, Sarah Larsen (2019) gives a step-by-step guide for how she uses her visualiser in class, which provides a really detailed grounding for less confident NQTs. It might be interesting to ask your mentee to read the blog post and then to come together and discuss how this is different from their own practice and why. Leading on from this, a useful exercise may be to reflect on how they have used worked examples or live modelling in their own lessons and the impact this has had on student understanding or the quality of student work (see pages 82–83).

Scaffolding and breaking down complex tasks into processes can sometimes be a difficult task, so using visual diagrams or representations might help. When beginning to plan for a week, ask your mentee to write down in the middle of an A3 piece of paper what skills or knowledge they want their class to have by the end of that series of lessons, and around it what tasks or activities they need to do to acquire the skills or knowledge. The usefulness of academic research on issues such as cognitive load theory is only relevant to classroom teachers if they can use it to help them with practical day-to-day teaching and improving student outcomes. It is about making the theory work for you. Sometimes it can be difficult to make these connections, therefore it's important to think about what guidance and support will be needed by your mentee and what that looks like in your subject.

C/W

How does Roth Estabish a Dystopian Setting?   25/2/20

Citizens have a fear of the   removes their
outside world.   aggressive   humanity/
                    plosives   personality
                            reason

Getting in
or
getting out.   Dauntless' "primary purpose
        is to guard the fence that
        surrounds / our city"   restricted?
                        protected?
cut off
isolated   protect
            from what?   fear
                    fear

Roth establishes a dystopian setting by creating a
clear sense that citizens have a fear of the
outside world. In the society built up of factions,
Dauntless' 'primary purpose' is only to 'guard'
a 'fence' that 'surrounds' the city in which
they live. Firstly, an aggressive tone is created
through the plosives Roth uses in describing
Dauntless' 'purpose'. This highlights the sense of
fear as it makes the phrase seem powerful and
assertive. Furthermore, the ~~the~~ lexical choice
of 'purpose' strips Dauntless of their personality
and humanity, furthering the sense of a dystopian
setting.

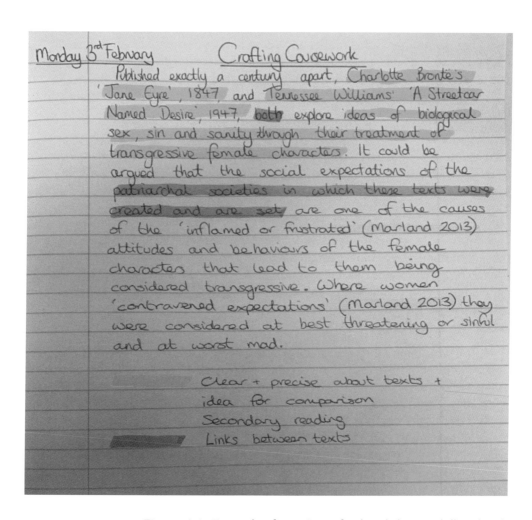

Monday 3rd February   Crafting Coursework
Published exactly a century apart, Charlotte Brontë's
'Jane Eyre', 1847, and Tennessee Williams' 'A Streetcar
Named Desire', 1947, both explore ideas of biological
sex, sin and sanity through their treatment of
transgressive female characters. It could be
argued that the social expectations of the
patriarchal societies in which these texts were
created and are set are one of the causes
of the 'inflamed or frustrated' (Marland 2013)
attitudes and behaviours of the female
characters that lead to them being
considered transgressive. Where women
'contravened expectations' (Marland 2013) they
were considered at best threatening or sinful
and at worst mad.

            Clear + precise about texts +
            idea for comparison
            Secondary reading
            Links between texts

Figure 4.1. Examples from @missfordenglish's modelling book

Head of English Gary Hammonds (2018) used some of the research he was doing on cognitive load theory to produce scaffolds for his students during essay writing, which can be extremely daunting to novice students when doing it from scratch. He wanted to break it down, so he gave them a task where he challenged them to explore different characters' responses to the death of Eva Smith in *An Inspector Calls* (Figure 4.2). After giving them a full model and some hints and quotations, he reduced the scaffolding to just hints and then withdrew the scaffolding altogether as the students gained more mastery. He includes many examples of scaffolds and models on his blog and talks about the process of developing mastery for students and when to take the supports away. Even for non-English specialists, there are ideas that can be adapted to other curriculum areas (see pages 86–87).

A longer-term project for your early career teacher may be to work on metacognitive strategies with their classes, so they are able to more successfully plan, monitor and evaluate. This is not a quick win – and embedding these processes will take time if they are to be embedded deeply and meaningfully. The EEF's *Metacognition and Self-Regulated Learning: Guidance Report* (2018c) is an invaluable document as it sets out seven clear recommendations, summarises the research in a clear way and, most importantly, gives ideas and guidance for how teachers can use it in their classrooms. The section on explicit instruction (p. 12) is particularly useful as it explains in simple terms how to guide students to plan their own work, by providing examples of effective teacher questions which can aid the development of their metacognitive reflection.

If you ask your mentee to bring along a lesson plan to one of your sessions, they could demonstrate the kind of metacognitive questions they would employ at each stage of the lesson: planning, monitoring and evaluation. The planning stage is when prior knowledge would be activated and any worked examples could be demonstrated. This is the exposition part of the lesson, where the correct knowledge needs to be imparted and modelled to students and any initial misconceptions addressed. During the monitoring stage, the teacher will emphasise the progress made, while also providing more challenge if needed and checking motivation. In the final evaluation stage, the teacher encourages the students to evaluate their progress and how successful they were, and also to reflect on what strategies they can take away from the learning to use again. Planning questions like this will ensure that your mentee is really prompting students to think about the different processes and stages of their own learning, which will set them in good stead to become more independent learners.

Questioning is such a vital component of high quality pedagogy that it is worth exploring different questioning strategies with your mentee throughout the year, so they can find out which ones work for them but also so they have these strategies stored away to use when needed. One of the types of questioning, which was discussed in the research section and informed some of the planning of the Early Career Framework, is dialogic questioning, where questions are more open, philosophical and challenging and promote critical thinking. As a newer teacher, it can be uncomfortable when you ask these kinds of questions, particularly when you are being observed, as it often takes students longer to think about them and articulate their answers, which can make it seem as if they don't know. Getting used to the wait time when more developed answers are required – and embracing the silences – takes experience. When we feel uncomfortable we are likely to want to fill the space, instead of seeing it as valuable thinking time during which students are formulating a quality answer.

Robin Alexander's *A Dialogic Teaching Companion* (2020), provides a framework and a suggested professional development programme for implementing dialogic teaching. One of the things that continuously came up in the focus group research was how new teachers enjoyed reading books alongside their mentors and having professional conversations about how they could influence their pedagogy. If you choose to read this book together, you could trial using dialogic questions and teaching methods over a term and measure the impact. If your mentee wants a challenge, they could then present their findings to the rest of the department and deliver some small-scale CPD.

Of course, there is a place for closed questions, particularly when assessing prior knowledge. Closed questions can be vital in providing information to the teacher on what the students already know, which will then feed into their planning. Recall quizzes and multiple-choice tests provide valuable assessment details about who has grasped the topic and what needs to be retaught or developed further to aid understanding. Used properly, these types of activities can also reduce teacher marking load as they can be used as a diagnostic tool in a live and responsive way. Sometimes these types of questions are referred to as 'hinge questions', as it is the part of the lesson when you need to shut the door and reteach a concept or open the door and send students off with limited guidance to complete a task more independently. The responses to these questions will give your mentee information and evidence about what they and their students need to do next.

Responses to the death of Eva Smith

Mr Birling

Mr Birling represents the older generation of British society, and he also represents capitalist and conservative views. He hears of what happens to Eva after he sacks her from his works and his response is: 'it happened more than eighteen months ago – nearly two years ago – obviously it has nothing whatever to do with the wretched girl's suicide'.

Even when he learns about the negative consequences of his behaviour, he doesn't accept responsibility. He is unwilling to change. Priestley is worried that this is true of older people in British society, and of the capitalists and the conservatives; he worries, in 1945, that they won't want to change. He says: 'I can't accept any responsibility. If we are all responsible for everything that happened to everybody we'd had anything to do with, it would be very awkward, wouldn't it?' This selfish attitude is typical of businesspeople, who are often concerned more with profits than the well-being of their workers.

Sheila

In your exercise book, write an explanation of how Sheila reacts to the death of Eva Smith. Sheila represents the younger generation of British society in 1945. Priestley hoped they would change society for the better. Sheila also grows to represent the socialist values that Priestley endorsed.

You should try to include the following quotations:

- 'But these girls aren't cheap labour – they're people!'
- '(rather distressed) Sorry! It's just that I can't help thinking about this girl – destroying herself so horribly.'
- 'I felt rotten about it at the time, and now I feel a lot worse.'
- 'If I could help her now, I would.'
- 'I'll never do it again to anybody.'

Gerald

In your exercise book, write an explanation of how Gerald reacts to the death of Eva Smith.

Gerald is almost 'trapped' between the generations. Some of the things he says suggest that, like Sheila, he cares about Eva Smith and the situation of working class people in general. Other things suggest that, like Mr Birling, he is more concerned with individualism, business and profits.

Use your copies of the text to find the evidence to talk about Gerald and how he reacts to Eva's death.

Priestley gives Birling all of these views, and uses dramatic irony to undermine them. Priestley makes Birling say things like 'unsinkable' in relation to the *Titanic* and 'the Germans don't want war'. Because the audience know these claims are wrong, they are less likely to trust Birling's views on other things.

Key dates

1912 – the play is set, the *Titanic* sinks

1914 – the Germans are involved in the start of the First World War

1918 – First World War ends

1939 – Second World War starts

1945 – Second World War ends, the play is written

Mrs Birling

Use your copies of the text, all of your notes and everything you know about the character to write an explanation of how Mrs Birling reacts to the death of Eva Smith.

Key vocabulary

materialistic – interested in physical belongings and wealth more than morality.

dramatic irony – when the audience members know things which the characters do not.

compassion – concern for the situation of others; pity for people worse off than yourself.

Figure 4.2. Scaffolding example for J. B. Priestley's *An Inspector Calls* (Hammond, 2018)

You can demonstrate how to use the data from closed questions on quizzes to inform planning by asking the new teacher to bring some results to a meeting and then explore together what difficulties the students might be experiencing, and anticipating and planning how to tackle them. The hinge questioning prompt in Figure 4.3 may help to steer this discussion. We are all experts in our subjects, but it can sometimes be difficult to understand our topics through the lens of a novice. This is the major difference between subject and pedagogical knowledge; to assist your NQT in improving their pedagogy, you need to encourage them to think about the best ways of imparting their subject knowledge to students, and what level of mastery they will accept from students before they feel it is time to move on. It is worth inviting your NQT into one of your lessons where you can demonstrate that there will be times when not all of the class are ready to move on at the same time. Remember, you can move on to a new concept or topic if 80% of the class are ready and set them some independent work, while you can then model how to scaffold and recap with the other students, or use the students who have mastered the concept as peer teachers. This is the reality of life in the classroom and it is healthy for new teachers to see this (see Figure 4.3).

There are many other different types of questioning techniques which are all useful in certain classroom scenarios. Unfortunately, the scope of this book is not wide enough to conduct a thorough exploration of them all in the depth and detail they deserve. However, Alex Quigley (2012) has written an excellent blog post about different questioning types. It is well worth reading and could be used as a reflective tool to complete an audit, after a week's teaching, on the kinds of questions your mentee used in their lessons and how they could be used more appropriately.

Finally, as stated in the literature review earlier in the chapter, collaborative working in groups can increase learners' success, but it is important that you support your mentee with the logistics of how to best group students so they are able to work together successfully. There are many journals about the science behind grouping, but for busy teachers the EEF's toolkit on collaborative learning (2018g) offers some straightforward guidance that teachers can use. They stress firstly that groups need the opportunity to practise working together and that training them to work together effectively takes time. This is a crucial message to stress to new teachers because if it is a disaster the first time they attempt it, they need to be secure in the knowledge that it is worth trying again.

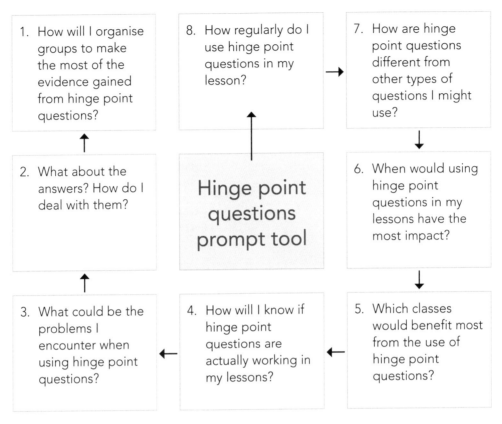

1. How will I organise groups to make the most of the evidence gained from hinge point questions?

2. What about the answers? How do I deal with them?

3. What could be the problems I encounter when using hinge point questions?

8. How regularly do I use hinge point questions in my lesson?

Hinge point questions prompt tool

4. How will I know if hinge point questions are actually working in my lessons?

7. How are hinge point questions different from other types of questions I might use?

6. When would using hinge point questions in my lessons have the most impact?

5. Which classes would benefit most from the use of hinge point questions?

Figure 4.3. How to use hinge point questions

It is essential that group tasks are carefully designed so that it is effective for students to work together on them; if not, some individuals will disengage and just work alone. Giving students specific roles may help with this, so they are all encouraged to contribute and share their ideas. As a mentor, you will need to consider what professional development your mentee needs in order to be able to support this approach: does their behaviour management need work, or perhaps their understanding of students' abilities using observations during feedback? If you are able to identify this and support the new teacher in this area, you will begin to equip them with the skills and the confidence to use group work in their lessons.

Chapter 4: Summary

Identify goal:

To develop skills of planning and teaching well-structured lessons which can transform students' knowledge, capabilities and beliefs about their own learning. Effective lessons will introduce new material in steps, while linking to previous topics and providing models and scaffolds to help students apply new ideas. Students should be explicitly taught metacognitive strategies which are linked to the subject. Skilful questioning and grouping should also be used. Homework should be meaningful and improve student outcomes.

Evaluate and reflect on the standard:

- Does the NQT now have an understanding about the ways that effective lessons are structured?
- Ask them to rate their confidence and identify areas where they need more support.
- Create an action plan for further reading and next steps to develop their skills.

Apply the learning:

- Use ideas from cognitive load theory about breaking down learning into processes and stages, and collaboratively plan a series of lessons, complete with scaffolding which gradually decreases as students master the skills and knowledge to undertake the task more independently.
- Encourage the NQT to trial different questioning techniques, including dialogic questioning, and assess the impact on engagement and effort.
- After reading Quigley's (2012) blog post on question types, organise for the NQT to observe staff across the curriculum with a focus on question types and how these are deployed.
- Use the EEF's (2018g) teacher toolkit on collaborative learning to guide your NQT on how to group pupils and monitor motivation, attainment and behaviour.

Standard 4 – Plan and teach well-structured lessons

Come up with a plan:

- Explore the foundational content knowledge that needs to be taught for each unit together, so the NQT is clear on expositions.
- Begin to compile collaboratively a list of resources and ideas for measuring student understanding and prior knowledge.
- Arrange meetings with other members of the department to understand what misconceptions and potential pitfalls students may have.
- Together start to develop ideas and resources for homework using spaced learning, challenge and choice.
- Buy an exercise book for your mentee so they can work on their planning models.

Learn together:

- Read and then discuss the short article by Rosenshine (2012) which gives practical tips on how lessons could be structured to maximise progress and impact.
- Both read Larsen's (2019) blog post and explore how she has written down the metacognitive processes she uses when modelling and completing worked examples. Film yourselves modelling and then try to write down the processes you both go through.
- Look at the EEF's (2018c) report on metacognition (especially p. 12) and together plan the types of questions that could be used by the NQT during each stage.

Chapter 5

Adapt teaching

Adaptive teaching (Standard 5 – Adapt teaching)

Learn that ...	Learn how to ...
1. Pupils are likely to learn at different rates and to require different levels and types of support from teachers to succeed. 2. Seeking to understand pupils' differences, including their different levels of prior knowledge and potential barriers to learning, is an essential part of teaching. 3. Adapting teaching in a responsive way, including by providing targeted support to pupils who are struggling, is likely to increase pupil success. 4. Adaptive teaching is less likely to be valuable if it causes the teacher to artificially create distinct tasks for different groups of pupils or to set lower expectations for particular pupils.	**Develop an understanding of different pupil needs, by:** • *Identifying pupils who need new content further broken down.* • *Making use of formative assessment.* • *Working closely with the special educational needs co-ordinator (SENCO) and special education professionals and the designated safeguarding lead.* • *Using the SEND Code of Practice, which provides additional guidance on supporting pupils with SEND effectively.* **Provide opportunity for all pupils to experience success, by:** • *Adapting lessons, whilst maintaining high expectations for all, so that all pupils have the opportunity to meet expectations.*

Adaptive teaching (Standard 5 – Adapt teaching)

Learn that ...	Learn how to ...
5. Flexibly grouping pupils within a class to provide more tailored support can be effective, but care should be taken to monitor its impact on engagement and motivation, particularly for low attaining pupils. 6. There is a common misconception that pupils have distinct and identifiable learning styles. This is not supported by evidence and attempting to tailor lessons to learning styles is unlikely to be beneficial. 7. Pupils with special educational needs or disabilities are likely to require additional or adapted support; working closely with colleagues, families and pupils to understand barriers and identify effective strategies is essential.	• *Balancing input of new content so that pupils master important concepts.* • *Making effective use of teaching assistants [TAs].* **Meet individual needs without creating unnecessary workload, by:** • *Making use of well-designed resources (e.g. textbooks).* • *Planning to connect new content with pupils' existing knowledge or providing additional pre-teaching if pupils lack critical knowledge.* • *Building in additional practice or removing unnecessary expositions.* • *Reframing questions to provide greater scaffolding or greater stretch.* • *Considering carefully whether intervening within lessons with individuals and small groups would be more efficient and effective than planning different lessons for different groups of pupils.* **Group pupils effectively, by:** • *Applying high expectations to all groups, and ensuring all pupils have access to a rich curriculum.* • *Changing groups regularly, avoiding the perception that groups are fixed.* • *Ensuring that any groups based on attainment are subject specific.*

> **Adaptive teaching (Standard 5 – Adapt teaching)**
>
> **Notes**
>
> *Learn that …* statements are informed by the best available educational research.
>
> *Learn how to …* statements are drawn from a wider evidence base including both academic research and additional guidance from expert practitioners.

Why is this standard important? What does the research say?

In the previous chapter, planning was the focus of great teaching. Much of the research and guidance we examined focused on the need to plan, structure and sequence lessons carefully. Although planning is important, teaching is a dynamic profession and there is a need to be flexible and sometimes change or deviate from what you are teaching in reaction to things that happen in your classroom. Teachers have to be adaptive. This can be difficult when you are learning to teach, because deviating from a plan can seem akin to dropping a security blanket; ensuring that every student is able to make progress and being aware of the needs of individuals takes skill, practice and support from mentors. The fact is that even though many of the classes your NQT will be teaching are streamed and largely made up of students with similar prior attainment scores, they are nevertheless still likely to learn at different rates and require different levels and types of support in order to succeed. An essential part of being a good teacher is working to understand students' levels of prior knowledge and whether they have any barriers to learning; when these are discovered, teaching can be adapted to respond to these barriers and targeted support can be provided for those who are struggling. Doing this is likely to increase student success, as we know that the quality of schools can be somewhat determined by the way teachers respond to cognitive differences between students and how well they adapt their teaching to take account of individual student needs (Hamre and Pianta, 2005). Novice teachers may find this difficult because they need to develop advanced professional skills such as differentiation before they are able to do this (van de Grift, 2007; van de Grift et al., 2011; Maulana et al., 2015).

Differentiation has been a buzz word in education for over a decade, but it has become so overused that its meaning has become somewhat hazy and all-encompassing. For the purpose of this book, Tomlinson et al.'s (2003: 120) definition will be used: it is when 'teachers proactively modify curricula, teaching methods, resources, learning activities, and student products to address the diverse needs of individual students and small groups of students to maximize the learning opportunity for each student in a classroom'. It is not spending hours creating distinct tasks for different groups of students or setting certain students challenges and others not. It is not producing three objectives using the word stems 'all', 'must', 'some' and getting the students to spend half of their learning time copying them out. Differentiation doesn't mean that we have lower expectations of students; it means that we find the sweet spot in a lesson where we have high expectations and a level of challenge for all, but we also ensure that, with teacher support, all students have the opportunity to meet expectations.

It could be argued that differentiation has spawned more fads than any other classroom practice: the framing and copying of lesson objectives, bolt-on challenges on every PowerPoint slide, different permutations of tasks and worksheets. Yet perhaps the biggest differentiation myth, which worryingly still seems to persist in some schools, is learning styles. When I trained in the late 2000s, ascertaining what a student's preferred way of learning was seemed to be all the rage. I recall a session at university where we were all furnished with a questionnaire and asked to use them on our school placements later that week, after which we could tailor the activities in the lesson to match our students' learning styles. Of course, planning three different alternatives for every task is completely unsustainable and, what is more, there is absolutely no evidence that it makes a difference to student progress. Every few years the debate seems to open up again: David Didau (2011) refers to it as a 'a rusting can of worms' that keeps returning to become a 'wriggling mess … crawling all over the educational Twittersphere'.

Of course, nobody is claiming that individuals do not have a way that they prefer to learn, but as the EEF state: 'There is very limited evidence for any consistent set of learning "styles" that can be used reliably to identify genuine differences in the learning needs of young people, and evidence suggests that it is unhelpful to assign learners to groups or categories on the basis of a supposed learning style.'[1] Consequently, if busy teachers are looking for strategies that will improve progress and enable all students to succeed, it is not worth wasting time designing tasks which superficially seem to encompass visual, auditory, reading/writing and kinaesthetic learning styles. As Didau (2016) observes: 'the myth is that our preferences for experiencing information presented in a particular mode, or style, leads to improved outcomes. It doesn't.' What is dangerous is the fact that by focusing on learning styles, educators may 'neglect research on learning for which there is solid scientific

---

1 See https://educationendowmentfoundation.org.uk/evidence-summaries/teaching-learning-toolkit/learning-styles.

support' (Willingham, 2010: 35). As Pashler et al. (2008: 10) conclude: 'at present, there is no adequate evidence base to justify incorporating learning styles assessments into general educational practice. Thus, limited education resources would be better devoted to adopting other educational practices that have a strong evidence base, of which there are an increasing number.' Willingham's (2010) paper is clear, concise and summarises the research on learning styles in an easily digestible way; it is well worth signposting it to your NQT to aid their understanding of this issue.

Although there will be times when all students need extra help or support to succeed, those with special educational needs and disabilities (SEND) are likely to require additional or adapted support in lessons. For new teachers, it is vital that the barriers to learning for these students are identified swiftly and that effective strategies are identified and adhered to. As the range of different special educational needs is vast, it is useful to approach each child as an individual, but there is a lot of research already available on useful strategies for students with particular needs. Some research by Davis et al. (2004) explored the strategies and approaches that schools could employ to help students with additional needs and uncovered some useful findings. The review found that when teaching children with SEND, a multi-method approach is the most promising: when teachers use a combination of strategies it produces more powerful effects than when a single strategy solution is deployed. The report also recognised that quality of teaching is an important factor in determining the success of those with additional needs. However, although special educational knowledge is important, a lot of the strategies mentioned in the research are similar to those that may be used to teach all children well. Therefore, if schools have a drive to improve the quality of teaching and learning as a whole, 'some children would not need to be identified as having special educational needs' (Davis et al., 2004: 8).

There are a wealth of resources and studies online which highlight best practice when it comes to adapting your teaching to best support students with SEND; some of these have been collated later in this chapter. Davis et al.'s (2004) extensive research also highlights some useful findings for the areas of 'need' which are identified in the *SEND Code of Practice* (Department for Education, 2014b). All of these strategies are based on evidence, but how they are applied will differ across different school phases and contexts. As we know, teaching involves making professional judgements and being a reflective practitioner, or as Schön (1986: 36) calls it: 'reflection in action', which involves drawing on your knowledge and analysing what works from the research. It is normal to experiment with strategies from a range of evidence informed theories and strategies, guided by your own principles as an educator. The strategies and approaches which are linked to specific forms of SEN in Table 5.1 are ones that can be easily adapted for use in the new teacher's classroom and may even improve your own practice as a mentor.

Table 5.1. Strategies and approaches to use with specific forms of SEN (adapted from Davis et al., 2004)

Special educational need	Strategy and approach
Communication and interaction (Speech and language communication needs, severe and profound learning difficulties, autistic spectrum disorders)	• Early identification and intervention is key. • Involvement of parents and families in a collaborative partnership. • Collaborative working with other agencies using a child centred approach. • Teaching approaches that adopt additional visual reinforcement strategies to supplement verbal instruction. • An emphasis on teaching language and cognitive processes, and the strategies needed for effective generalisation.
Cognition and learning (A primary difficulty in academic learning, typically in aspects of attention, memory, problem-solving, reasoning, transfer of learning, language and literacy, specific learning difficulties or a syndrome, e.g. Down's Syndrome)	• There is a need for explicit, comprehensive and integrated teaching of different aspects of reading – phonological, syntactic and semantic – and reading should be linked to spelling and writing. • Many children will need repetitive and cumulative learning opportunities together with metacognitive development.

Special educational need	Strategy and approach
	<ul><li>There should be careful and ongoing assessment linked with teaching, avoiding prescriptive and inflexible programme delivery.</li><li>Procedural facilitators like planning sheets, writing frames, story mapping and teacher modelling of cognitive strategies are useful.</li><li>Elaborated higher-order questioning and dialogue between teachers and pupils.</li><li>A focus on developing talking, listening and thinking skills, not just literacy skills.</li><li>Organisational and physical features of the classroom should not be distracting.</li><li>Cooperative group learning can produce positive academic and social outcomes for pupils.</li><li>Home-school literacy programmes can be used for interventions.</li></ul>
Behaviour, emotional and social development (Emotional/psychiatric disturbance, a reaction to outward circumstances, attention deficit hyperactivity disorder)	<ul><li>Peers are a valuable resource as part of a behaviour management programme, like peer mentoring or a buddy system.</li><li>Cognitive-behavioural approaches that teach self-monitoring, self-instruction, anger management and self-reinforcement skills are effective.</li><li>Positive behaviour reduction strategies appear to be effective in increasing on-task behaviour.</li></ul>

Special educational need	Strategy and approach
	• Combinations of approaches are more effective in facilitating positive social, emotional and behavioural outcomes than single approaches alone. • Parents need to be actively involved as partners in their child's education, and in presenting a unified front in portraying behavioural, emotional and social difficulties in terms that provide children with a sense of empowerment.
Sensory and/or physical (Visually impaired, hearing impaired, multi-sensory impaired or physically disabled)	• Participatory/active learning methods such as cued speech – especially if used both at home and at school – are more likely to help students use phonological coding. • Creating an atmosphere which encourages the integration of emotional and social development with academic and cognitive growth. • Physical education as a means of bridging the therapeutic/ educational divide for students with physical disabilities. • Strategies focusing on developing communication through personal agency, such as setting personal learning targets. • The use of computer software for children with visual impairment.

Formative assessment is a reliable way to ascertain whether teachers need to adapt their teaching, and it also helps to identify students who may need extra support or to have content further broken down. Paul Black and Dylan Wiliam (1998) define it as any form of assessment that teachers or students undertake which provides feedback, that is then used to meet students' needs by adapting teaching. Between 2015 and 2017, the EEF conducted a study where they worked with a number of primary and secondary schools which delivered a two-year intervention programme called Embedding Formative Assessment (EEF, 2018a). The teachers involved attended workshops where they shared new formative assessment ideas and fed back on their use of formative assessment techniques. At the end of the study, students in the schools made the equivalent of two additional months of progress in their Attainment 8 GCSE score and teachers felt that taking part in the programme and using more regular formative assessment strategies had improved their practice.

Wiliam proposes five effective formative assessment strategies and they each get a chapter in his book *Embedding Formative Assessment* (Wiliam and Leahy, 2015):

1. Clarifying, sharing and understanding learning intentions and success criteria.
2. Engineering effective discussion, tasks and activities that elicit evidence of learning.
3. Providing feedback that moves learning forward.
4. Activating students as learning resources for one another.
5. Activating students as owners of their own learning.

These strategies can be useful for guiding planning and formulating ideas for classroom activities. As he observes, 'there is intuitive appeal in using assessment to support instruction: assessment for learning rather than assessment of learning. We have to test our students for many reasons … such testing should be useful in guiding teaching' (Wiliam et al., 2005: 22). Using formative assessment in this way will help teachers plan how to connect new content with students' existing knowledge and also indicate when additional pre-teaching is needed when they lack the critical knowledge to progress. These strategies will be explored further in the 'How can I help my mentee meet this standard?' section of this chapter.

Consideration also needs to be given to the learner's journey: where do you want them to go? Where do they need to be? How will they get there? The role of the teacher, the peers and the learner are instrumental to this journey as there are certain roles and responsibilities that each has to undertake in order to make this journey possible. These are summed up in Figure 5.1.

Where is the learner now?

Teacher: Facilitating effective tasks and discussions that show evidence of learning.

Peers: Empowering students to be learning resources for one another.

Learners: Empowering students to be the drivers and architects of their own learning.

The learning journey

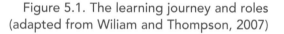

How can they get there?

Teacher: Providing feedback to help learners progress.

Peers: Empowering students to be learning resources for one another.

Learners: Empowering students to be the drivers and architects of their own learning.

Where is the learner going?

Teacher ⎤
⎥ Clarifying,
⎥ sharing and
Peer ⎥ understanding
⎥ learning
⎥ intentions.
Learner ⎦

Figure 5.1. The learning journey and roles (adapted from Wiliam and Thompson, 2007)

Finally, the way that students are grouped can have an effect on their progress. Many schools choose to sort students based on prior performance, as they are seeking to create a more homogeneous learning environment where the teacher can pitch to the correct level. However, according to the OECD (2015), students in lower ability groups often do not benefit as much as those in higher ability groups from this form of setting, as they have no high performing peers to be inspired by or learn from. As mentioned in Chapter 1, this can also lead to teachers subconsciously 'dumbing down' content and almost creating a glass ceiling of expectations, where they have preconceived views about what students of that level are capable of. Other schools teach in mixed-ability sets and teach to the top, using scaffolding as needed. This provides better opportunities for students to learn from one another. As Tom Sherrington (2017a: 156) says: 'I've always found that it is a win-win to cater explicitly for the highest attaining students in any groups; to "teach to the top", pitching every lesson and the general thrust of every unit of work to stretch them.' Creating a culture of academia in every set is key. Mark Enser (2017) adds that 'what is needed instead is a culture of excellence that permeates every classroom, department and school; a focus not on simply getting the best grade, but on getting the best education and creating a lifelong passion for learning'.

There should not be the perception that groups and sets are fixed, or that if a student is in a lower or higher set for maths then this should be replicated across all subject disciplines. Although whether classes are set by ability is decided by the school, teachers can group students within their class to help them succeed and make progress. For example, with within-class ability grouping, teachers assign students to several smaller groups so they can base their instruction on filling in gaps in knowledge or correcting misconceptions. In a study by Steenbergen-Hu et al. (2016), it was revealed that the effects of within-class grouping on students' overall academic achievement was positive and statistically significant: it had at least a small positive impact on academic achievement, regardless of students' initial achievement or ability levels. Within-class groupings can also give students who may be struggling with class work role models if they are put into groups with higher attaining peers. Learners do identify themselves through a hierarchy of ability, and the various discourses around this can constrain students with the mindset that they are not as academic as others, resulting in lower confidence and motivation. This is demonstrated in some studies where students with lower prior attainment stated that they preferred being educated in more mixed attainment groups due to 'friendships, social mixing, and equality of learning opportunities' (Tereshchenko et al., 2019: 427).

Crucially, if students believe that settings and groupings are immovable, even if they make progress, they may develop a fixed mindset: the belief that their intelligence is stable and cannot be developed. Carol Dweck (2008) says: 'what students believe about their brains – whether they see their intelligence as something that's fixed or something that can grow and change – has profound effects on their motivation, learning, and school achievement'. Instead, we need to create a culture where the importance of hard work and practice is accentuated, and where we teach students that although people may differ in terms of their initial talents and aptitudes, everyone can change and grow through application and perseverance. There is evidence that students who have more of a growth mindset enjoy more positive outcomes, including higher academic achievement (Sisk et al., 2018); therefore, teaching to the top, cultivating a growth mindset and a 'can do' culture can help students to achieve and succeed in your subject.

Focus group findings

My mentor often came into my classroom just before the lesson I was nervous about started to reassure me that I was going to be okay, and I always went straight to her after the lesson, whether it was a good or bad one. I knew she would share my success happily if it had gone well and listen to me lament if I had to cry for how badly it had gone. I could not have asked for more.

A supportive presence and a shoulder to cry on, or one with whom to celebrate successes, is something that most participants spoke about when describing their mentors. There is no doubt that the NQT year can be an emotional rollercoaster, so it is important for a mentor to be there and for your mentee to know that you are available and willing to listen.

The participants were overwhelmingly positive about how their mentors had supported them in adapting their teaching and helping them to meet the needs of all their students. The teacher who made the observation above shared their experiences of the support they had been offered which was extremely comprehensive. Before the NQT started at the school, their mentor sent them their class lists, flagged up any SEND students and then opened up a channel of communication between them and the school's special educational needs and disabilities coordinator (SENDCO), as the teacher did not feel confident enough to reach out initially. The mentor later helped them to look through the schemes of learning and advised them to tailor certain lessons to individual classes, such as bespoke work booklets for a challenging, disengaged Year 10 class. This support continued, so that together they created regular booklets for this class, which established a sense of routine and made the NQT feel more confident to try the same for other groups too.

Another teacher spoke about how their mentor had modelled care plans and how to best use them to keep track of high need students, what to do for them specifically and whether it was working. They were also positive about the extensive range of resources that were already on the shared drive, as they felt that they provided a solid base which could be quickly and easily adapted. The same mentor provided many English as an additional language (EAL) resources to the new teacher, as there were a high number of EAL students in the school. The teacher was also able to regularly meet with the school's EAL lead, who could then feed back to them whether the work was appropriately pitched. This resulted in them feeling empowered enough to create their own resources using the expertise they had learned from their more expert colleague.

Some teachers felt that they improved gradually through a range of support but couldn't necessarily pinpoint what in particular their mentor did. One participant said: 'Much of the improvement came through focusing on how to engage and support a range of pupils, but this didn't mean I had to do masses of extra work. It was about listening to my mentor as a very experienced practitioner and going to talk to relevant people about specific pupils and their needs and taking that on board as well.' They felt that this was particularly effective support because when their mentor didn't know the answer they were able to point them in the right direction to find information or support. As well as being useful, this also demonstrated that mentors themselves are not the finished article, and this helped the early career teacher to realise that teaching is the kind of profession where professionals are always developing.

Another participant said that although their mentor was supportive, they felt a bit stifled by the way they were told to group students – to sit them in rigid ability groups all lesson, every lesson. The NQT did try to move the students around, but this was commented on by the mentor when they popped in to observe the lesson. However, they did talk the teacher through why they wouldn't do it that way and added reasons why they should stick to ability groups, so the teacher had felt that their mentor trusted their judgement.

There were some teachers who felt that they hadn't really been taught how to meet the needs of students and had been left to jump in at the deep end without any armbands. With one NQT, it was noticed that some students were struggling during a lesson observation and their mentor commented that they hadn't provided scaffolds to help them access the task. This was not something they had discussed previously, however, so they had not thought about how they could do this in their subject – religious studies. This then became a focus and, after observing other colleagues and collaboratively planning some resources, they felt much more confident.

How can I help my mentee meet this standard?

It is important that new teachers are encouraged and supported to develop an understanding of the different needs in their classes. Initially, this can be done via exploring the data and information that is held on students, such as any SEND or safeguarding/pastoral information that can be shared. This can be especially difficult when this type of information isn't shared. I recall an incident from my own early practice when a student was moved into my class without prior warning, and in an effort to get to know them, I asked them whether they had any brothers or sisters who had previously attended the school that I may know. I hoped this would build some kind of rapport and put the student more at ease. They replied that they didn't know whether they had any siblings and, not thinking, I made a jokey comment along the lines of, how could they not know whether they had any siblings. I found out later on that their only sibling had tragically died earlier that year; as you can imagine, I was mortified. This is why communication is so vital and, as a new teacher, collaborating with other colleagues in your department and across the school can fill in gaps about students and their needs that data cannot necessarily capture.

TAs are a valuable source of information and expertise, but your mentee may need help with how to deploy them most effectively. In their report on how to make the best use of TAs, the EEF (2018b) make seven key recommendations to maximise their impact. The report is well worth a read to give your NQT some ideas about how to utilise them in lessons. The results of the report are clear: poor TA deployment has a negative effect on attainment, whereas effective TA deployment has a positive impact. Some easy strategies that your mentee can try are to ensure that their TAs are fully prepared for their role in the classroom by sharing the content and aims of the lesson with them in advance and directing them to the students with whom they should be working. They should be made aware of the key concepts, facts and information being taught before the lesson and also the skills to be learned, applied, practised or extended.

In addition, it is important that TAs are there to help students develop their independent learning skills and manage their own learning, so they shouldn't be focusing their energies on writing the students' work for them or giving them too much assistance. The report states:

TAs should be trained to avoid prioritising task completion and instead concentrate on helping pupils develop ownership of tasks. TAs should aim to give pupils the least amount of help first. They should allow sufficient wait time, so pupils can respond to a question or attempt the stage of a task independently. TAs should intervene appropriately when pupils demonstrate they are unable to proceed. (EEF, 2018b: 15)

In summary, the report states that to achieve more student autonomy and independence, TAs should avoid just correcting students and instead move towards modelling, using clues and prompting before they encourage them to self-scaffold and complete a task.

Another way that your mentee can use TAs is to deliver high quality, one-to-one and small group support using structured interventions. According the EEF, this is the area of research which shows the strongest evidence for TAs having a positive impact, with results demonstrating a consistent impact on student attainment of approximately three to four additional months of progress over an academic year. However, these positive effects are only observed when TAs work in structured settings with high quality support and training. When this isn't the case, and the groups are more informal, there are no recorded positive outcomes. There are some useful case studies of evidence based intervention sessions on the EEF website, but these are not exhaustive. The key is that these sessions are well resourced and structured and that TAs closely follow the plan and script. It would be useful to read the EEF's report together and specifically include the deployment of the TA in your NQT's planning, so they can identify how to use the recommendations in the classroom. This could then be a focus in their weekly observation. In addition, the mentee could observe other staff, with a focus on how they deploy their TAs, and this could be cross-referenced with the report.

Identifying which students need more support or intervention can be achieved by using different formative assessment strategies in lessons. As discussed previously, Dylan Wiliam and Siobhan Leahy (2015) outline five essential strategies for formative assessment which teachers should integrate into their lessons. Experienced practitioners will use these strategies regularly, often without really thinking about it. However, early career teachers may need more support to do this, so to help them you can make links between the strategies and some of Rosenshine's principles that were discussed in Chapter 3. Table 5.2 demonstrates how closely these interlink, so this table can be used as a discussion prompt or to reflect and evaluate on lessons that have already taken place. It can also be used as a focus for early career teachers to observe others and to seek out these strategies when they are demonstrated and modelled by more experienced practitioners.

Table 5.2. Connections between Wiliam's formative assessment strategies and Rosenshine's principles of instruction

Wiliam's strategies for formative assessment	Rosenshine's principles	What does this look like in the classroom?
Clarifying understanding and sharing learning intentions	• Learning intentions • Self-regulation and metacognition • Criteria for excellence	• Provide models and scaffolds for more difficult tasks. • Teach students the metacognition cycle (e.g. evaluating strengths and weaknesses, planning approach and reflecting). • Share the success criteria and what different degrees of success look like.
Engineering effective classroom discussions, tasks and activities that elicit evidence of learning	• Question design • Responsive teaching and adaptive planning	• Use different types of questions, such as quizzing and multiple-choice, to ascertain prior knowledge or correct misconceptions after teaching. • Ask questions and perform knowledge checks. Check student understanding through diagnostic tools, such as questioning where as many students as possible are involved. Tasks, discussions and activities are also useful.
Providing feedback that moves learners forward	• Self-assessment	• Guide student practice and train them to redraft and evaluate their work against success criteria.

Wiliam's strategies for formative assessment	Rosenshine's principles	What does this look like in the classroom?
	• Feedback needs to be specific • Feedback needs to be actioned	• Give targets that are actionable and specific and give students the chance to redraft, repeat, rehearse, respond and revisit. • Make sure it is understandable and that students see the value of it and are motivated.
Activating students as learning resources for one another	• Strong routines and meaningful dialogue • Structured roles to support one another	• Think, pair, share activities – train students how to do this. • Use Hattie's (2009) reciprocal teaching ideas to give students roles (e.g. summarising, question generator, clarifying, predicting).
Activating students as owners of their own learning	• Self-regulation and metacognition • Forming schema • Big picture	• Set learning goals, plan tasks, monitor and evaluate the success of tasks. • Help students to build, change and grow their schemas with new knowledge. • Encourage students to look at the bigger picture and how their learning fits into this. Encourage them to explore how they can get there.

Empowering students so they have true ownership of their own learning involves making them aware of the bigger picture. It is important that new teachers have a strong understanding of the course and curriculum and what students are studying towards, so they can impart this to them. For example, they could give students access to a long-term plan or overview before they focus on particular topics, exam content or skills. This map could be displayed in the classroom or stuck into books so the students can keep track of their progress during the learning journey and plan their own next steps. Not only will this help them to become increasingly independent, but it will also give early career teachers a clear sense of purpose and direction.

As discussed earlier in this chapter, good differentiation is not about producing different versions of resource sheets or offering some students challenge and extension tasks, while others are offered 'easier' versions of activities. Not only does this fail to meet the individual needs of students, but it also creates huge amounts of unnecessary work at a time when an NQT is still getting used to balancing a heavy workload. For a while, textbooks were out of fashion in education and were seen as an old relic of a bygone age. But then, in 2013, then Education and Childcare Minister Liz Truss spoke about how great textbooks are and professed that they gave students reliable access to an agreed core of 'essential knowledge' about a subject, while also providing them with a sense of ownership about their learning. At the time, textbooks were only being used by 8% of teachers in England, while for educational overachievers, like Korea, 88% of teachers used them for instruction and 92% in China (Bircher, 2013). Yet, even with the growing use of technology in lessons, there is still evidence that students learn more effectively from print textbooks than from screens. In a review of research done since 1992, scientists found that students were able to better comprehend information in print from texts that were more than a page in length; this appears to be partly because scrolling has a disruptive effect on concentration levels (Singer and Alexander, 2017).

Textbooks can also be useful to teachers, particularly those who are just starting out as educators. In a study by Loewenberg Ball and Feiman-Nemser (1988), new teachers spoke about how they had been given the impression during training that to be a good teacher you had to make all your own resources. However, when they started teaching they found this difficult as they lacked the knowledge, skills and experience to create content completely from scratch. The study concluded that textbooks can be useful to new teachers and that they should be taught how to make use of good quality published curricular materials. Although this study is now quite dated, there is still a perception by some new teachers that I questioned about textbook use, and some in the focus group, who felt that it was lazy to use them. However, encouraging your new teacher to make use of ready-made resources may take the pressure off them for a bit and help to develop and supplement their subject knowledge.

What teachers can do is sometimes constrained by their context and the choices that have been made both in departments and across the whole school. However, one focus that new teachers can take ownership of is the level of challenge in their own classroom, because applying high expectations or teaching to the top will ensure that everyone can make progress and succeed. 'Teaching to the top' has become a buzz phrase in education, so it is worth asking your NQT what they think this looks like in their curriculum area: what are the high level skills a scholar in their subject needs to possess? Once you have discussed this and decided what they are, the teacher then needs to think about how they can help the students to learn these skills. The ideas they come up with from this discussion are the practical answers to what teaching to the top may mean in practice.

If students are striving for excellence, they need to know what this looks like through examples of student work or models that the teacher does live in front of the class, while simultaneously describing their thought processes. The good parts can then be discussed by the class, along with any parts that could be improved further. Once they are aware of how to complete a task, the students need to have a secure enough knowledge of the subject to be able to write about it in the depth required for excellence. If they do not have sufficient knowledge, their application will not be meaningful and the challenge will seem unattainable. This is why feedback is so important: if your mentee circulates around the room giving feedback as the students work, they will be more equipped to address any misconceptions or adapt their teaching to ensure that all their students are adequately challenged and supported.

In order to teach to the top, Tom Sherrington (2017b) states that teachers should plan every lesson or sequence of lessons with the highest attainers in mind and celebrate intellectual curiosity. He also adds that there should be a culture of academia in a classroom, so that it is seen as credible to do the 'nerdy' or 'geeky' tasks and that, even in lower sets, teachers should not dumb things down. This blog post is an excellent introduction to what having high expectations really means in practical terms and it also sets out the theories and research that underpin this idea. It contains many ideas for embedding challenge for all in lessons; the new teacher could plan a series of lessons including some of these activity ideas for one of their less able classes and then reflect on them in a later meeting with you. This will ensure that the NQT has some strategies they can use in future – regardless of what ability groupings they teach – so that all students have access to a rich curriculum.

Chapter 5: Summary

Identify goal:
To understand that students have different needs and are likely to learn at different rates and require different levels of support. Realise that teaching needs to be adapted in a responsive way and that, to do this, it may be necessary to work with the SENDCO and families to understand barriers to learning and identify strategies to help them progress.

Standard 5 – Adapt teaching

Evaluate and reflect on the standard:
- Does the NQT now have an understanding about the ways that lessons can be adapted to meet the needs of all learners?
- Ask them to rate their confidence and identify areas where they need more support.
- Create an action plan for further reading and next steps to develop their skills.

Apply the learning:
- Remind the NQT to meet their TA before lessons and to share key concepts, knowledge and learning intentions so they know where the students are headed and how best to support them.
- Encourage a culture of sharing so that resources are available for all to use in lessons; this includes high quality textbooks.
- Get the NQT to use success criteria and models of high level answers which can be used to demonstrate what good answers should look like.

Come up with a plan:

- Provide the necessary information so the NQT can research any issues relating to students in their class which may impact on their ability to learn. Help them to set up meetings with the pastoral team, the SENDCO and former teachers to support with this.
- Both read the EEF's (2018b) advice on deploying TAs and discuss what works and what to avoid in a mentoring meeting.
- Plan observations for your NQT to see how other teachers successfully use TAs in their lessons.
- Invite the NQT to observe you with a focus on how you use different forms of formative assessment to adapt teaching.

Learn together:

- Use the SEN guidance document from the Department for Education (2014b) and Table 5.1 to collaboratively plan activities and resources for lessons.
- Together plan a series of lessons where deployment and instructions to the TA are explicitly detailed.
- Discuss Wiliam and Leahy's (2015) five strategies for assessment and use Table 5.2, which links them to metacognition and Rosenshine's principles, to reflect on how they have been/can be used in lessons.
- Explore the department's long-term plan so that new teachers can see the strategic vision and learning journey and how their lessons fit into this.
- Define what it means to be a scholar in your subject and collect models that demonstrate what excellence is, which your NQT can then use in their lessons.

Chapter 6

Make accurate and productive use of assessment

Adaptive teaching (Standard 6 – Make accurate and productive use of assessment)	
Learn that …	**Learn how to …**
1. Effective assessment is critical to teaching because it provides teachers with information about pupils' understanding and needs. 2. Good assessment helps teachers avoid being over-influenced by potentially misleading factors, such as how busy pupils appear. 3. Before using any assessment, teachers should be clear about the decision it will be used to support and be able to justify its use. 4. To be of value, teachers use information from assessments to inform the decisions they make; in turn, pupils must be able to act on feedback for it to have an effect.	**Avoid common assessment pitfalls, by:** • *Planning formative assessment tasks linked to lesson objectives and thinking ahead about what would indicate understanding (e.g. by using hinge questions to pinpoint knowledge gaps).* • *Drawing conclusions about what pupils have learned by looking at patterns of performance over a number of assessments (e.g. appreciating that assessments draw inferences about learning from performance).* • *Choosing, where possible, externally validated materials, used in controlled conditions when required to make summative assessments.*

Adaptive teaching (Standard 6 – Make accurate and productive use of assessment)

Learn that ...	Learn how to ...
5. High quality feedback can be written or verbal; it is likely to be accurate and clear, encourage further effort and provide specific guidance on how to improve. 6. Over time, feedback should support pupils to monitor and regulate their own learning. 7. Working with colleagues to identify efficient approaches to assessment is important; assessment can become onerous and have a disproportionate impact on workload.	**Check prior knowledge and understanding during lessons, by:** • *Using assessments to check for prior knowledge and pre-existing misconceptions.* • *Structuring tasks and questions to enable the identification of knowledge gaps and misconceptions (e.g. by using common misconceptions within multiple choice questions).* • *Prompting pupils to elaborate when responding to questioning to check that a correct answer stems from secure understanding.* • *Monitoring pupil work during lessons, including checking for misconceptions.* **Provide high quality feedback, by:** • *Focusing on specific actions for pupils and providing time for pupils to respond to feedback.* • *Appreciating that pupils' responses to feedback can vary depending on a range of social factors (e.g. the message the feedback contains or the age of the child).* • *Scaffolding self-assessment by sharing model work with pupils, highlighting key details.*

Adaptive teaching (Standard 6 – Make accurate and productive use of assessment)	
Learn that …	**Learn how to …**
	• *Thinking carefully about how to ensure feedback is specific and helpful when using peer- or self-assessment.*
	Make marking manageable and effective, by:
	• *Recording data only when it is useful for improving pupil outcomes.*
	• *Working with colleagues to identify efficient approaches to marking and alternative approaches to providing feedback (e.g. using whole class feedback or well supported peer- and self-assessment).*
	• *Using verbal feedback during lessons in place of written feedback after lessons where possible.*
	• *Understanding that written marking is only one form of feedback.*
	• *Reducing the opportunity cost of marking (e.g. by using abbreviations and codes in written feedback).*
	• *Prioritising the highlighting of errors related to misunderstandings, rather than careless mistakes when marking.*
Notes	
Learn that … statements are informed by the best available educational research.	
Learn how to … statements are drawn from a wider evidence base including both academic research and additional guidance from expert practitioners.	

Why is this standard important?
What does the research say?

Effective assessment is one of the cornerstones of teaching; not only should it give teachers an indication of what levels a student is working at, but it should also inform planning and help teachers to understand individual students' needs. Assessment is defined as 'the systematic process of documenting and using empirical data on the knowledge, skill, attitudes, and beliefs to refine programs and improve student learning' (Allen, 2004). There are a wealth of different formats and types of assessment that teachers can use. However, the key to good assessment is whether the type chosen is valid to measure the learning outcome it has been used to assess – for example, if a learning outcome is focused on how to use ambitious vocabulary and language techniques for effect, a piece of descriptive writing might be a valid assessment.

One of the main types of assessment is summative, which is used to sum up a student's learning and achievement. This is sometimes described as a 'feedout' assessment as learners are provided with a grade which shows their competence. Summative assessments are sometimes external and often high stakes, in that they provide information which may act as 'performance indicators in appraising the work of teachers, departments, colleges and national systems of education' (Knight, 2001: 4). It could be argued that exam style summative assessments, particularly those that are marked externally, are more objective and reliable as they are largely free from implicit bias, as the examiners marking the papers do not know the students. However, for teaching purposes, formative assessment is often more useful, as it can identify more clearly what students need to do to improve their work, while also acting as a diagnostic tool for teachers who can identify misconceptions and barriers to learning, enabling them to plan carefully to help aid progress. The stakes do not seem as high with formative assessment, and there is an emphasis on providing useful feedback which moves on the learner. There is a place for both kinds of assessment, and benefits to each, but to be of genuine value, teachers need to be able to use assessment to inform the decisions they make in their teaching and students need to be able to act on the feedback it provides.

Some of the most seminal writing and theory on assessment comes from Paul Black and Dylan Wiliam's *Inside the Black Box: Raising Standards Through Classroom Assessment* (1998). When I was training to be a teacher, this book was a core text on the course; it aimed to raise standards of learning in classrooms by using the analogy of schools being like a 'black box'. The authors propose that certain inputs are fed in from the outside, such as management rules, external tests and pressure from parents, but that inside, it seems to be up to teachers to secure better outcomes by ensuring that learning improves. They acknowledge that this is a tough task and that it doesn't seem fair to pile this responsibility solely on teachers when they already have so much to balance. To make this easier, they suggest that teaching and learning has to be interactive – it is imperative that teachers understand the needs of their students so they can adapt their teaching and address them. They suggest that formative assessment is an excellent way to do this, whether this is assessment undertaken by a teacher or a student, which then provides information that can be used to give feedback and adapt the teaching to meet the needs of the students. This kind of assessment has often been grouped under the banner of assessment for learning, as it isn't just about assessing students' learning; the findings are directly feeding back into the learning, and shaping and moulding it into something which helps more students to succeed.

Research suggests that when coupled with a culture of success, formative assessment can help all students but can be particularly powerful with low achievers, especially when they gain a clear understanding of where they have gone wrong and are given achievable targets about how to fix it (Black and Wiliam, 2001). In addition, self-assessment and peer assessment can add a new dimension to formative assessment, with the proviso that students have a clear picture of the targets they need to attain and the rationale for what excellence looks like. Black and Wiliam (2001: 7) claim that when students get this overview, they 'become more committed and more effective as learners: their own assessments become an object of discussion with their teachers and with one another, and this promotes even further that reflection on one's own ideas that is essential to good learning'. Yet it seems that the quality of feedback is of most importance. Sadler (1989) suggests that good student feedback has three elements: the desired goal, some evidence about where they are presently in relation to that goal, and an understanding of what they need to do to close the gap.

Of course, high quality feedback does not just need to be written; it can also be verbal. Written marking has always played a central role in the work of teachers in assessing progress and identifying misunderstandings, but the government made it a priority to reform marking policies after it was revealed in the 2014 Workload Challenge Survey that excessive marking loads were a key driver for teachers leaving the profession. For years, schools had been subscribing to the ideology that in order for written feedback to be thorough and robust, it had to be long and arduous – sometimes schools were even advocating time-consuming practices such as triple marking. Not only is this unsustainable, but it also seems to be more of a box ticking exercise which is used to look impressive to visitors, but does not necessarily move the students' learning forward. It has been claimed that feedback like this is unfocused and that when using written corrective feedback, less is more (Lee, 2019).

Furthermore, in *A Marked Improvement?*, Elliott et al. (2016) state that rewarding grades for every piece of work reduces the impact of marking and that the use of specific, actionable targets is more likely to increase progress. The review also advised that corrections of misunderstandings would be more useful if they were differentiated from careless mistakes through the use of hints or questions from the teacher, which would lead students to correct the underlying principles independently. In addition, the practice of acknowledgement marking is unlikely to enhance progress and that, instead, schools should mark less but what they do mark should be marked more usefully, giving students the time to consider and respond to it by improving their work. This review led to many schools rewriting their feedback policies to be more about feedback than marking – encompassing a range of different feedback tools, including verbal, peer and self-assessment.

In Hattie's (1999) meta-analysis on the effects of aspects of schooling on student achievement, it was revealed that the highest effect sizes involved students receiving feedback about a task and how to do it more effectively. He proposes a model for effective feedback (see Figure 6.1) which suggests that using feedback questions at four levels can enhance learning. These include the ideas of feeding up, feeding back and feeding forward; the journey needs to be clear in order for students to be able to monitor and regulate their own learning.

Dylan Wiliam (2017a) proposes that teachers should make feedback into detective work. For example, by not just stating what is wrong and moving on but by getting the students to be active participants and to respond and think about how to improve. For example, instead of circling all of the apostrophe errors, you could instead inform the student that there are three apostrophe errors on the page and they should find and correct them. He also stresses the importance of giving a reason for the feedback, especially if it could be conceived as critical. Feedback tools such as verbal feedback are useful, but they are most effective when 'teachers use assessment minute-by-minute and day-by-day as part of regular teaching, not as part of a monitoring process' (Wiliam, 2017a: 48). The immediacy of verbal feedback can be extremely quick and effective to set students on the right path.

Each feedback question works at four levels:

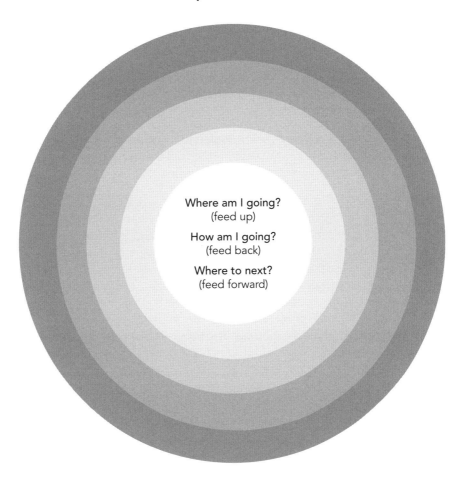

Where am I going?
(feed up)

How am I going?
(feed back)

Where to next?
(feed forward)

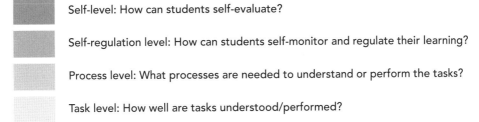

Self-level: How can students self-evaluate?

Self-regulation level: How can students self-monitor and regulate their learning?

Process level: What processes are needed to understand or perform the tasks?

Task level: How well are tasks understood/performed?

Figure 6.1. Effective feedback principles inspired
by Hattie's feedback model (1999)

Furthermore, research by University College London (2019) found that when accompanied by the reduction or removal of written feedback, verbal feedback doesn't negatively affect students' engagement or attainment. In fact, the engagement of disadvantaged students improved and there were also large examples of gains in their progress and attainment. Importantly, the time that teachers would normally spend on marking outside of lessons was more valuably reinvested in planning better lessons and improving student outcomes in this way. When used as feedback, the language of the mark scheme is often too abstract for students to understand, and the use of these criteria to assess work in lessons can be doubly confusing because learning is not linear. As Daisy Christodoulou (2017) states, 'what happens in the lesson is an "input", if you like, and what happens in the exam is an "output". It makes no sense to try to measure both on the same scale.'

Sometimes, the marking of assessments can become onerous – and this, in turn, has a disproportionate impact on workload, particularly when work is being assessed by a less experienced teacher who hasn't yet got to grips with the mark scheme and may not feel confident that their judgements are secure. Writing assessments are usually marked using prose descriptions of performance. Teachers then use these descriptors to guide their judgements and provide a grade using best fit. However, these descriptors are often very subjective, as a teacher's judgement on whether student work is 'compelling' or 'engaging' could be entirely different from another colleague's judgement. Christodoulou (2018) recognises that marking writing consistently is difficult and that to see how well students are doing and whether they are improving, teachers need a reliable method of assessing extended writing. She advocates comparative judgement, instead of the system of absolute judgement, where markers assess a pair of essays and judge which one is better. The judgement is more holistic and considers the overall quality of the writing; it is also a lot quicker than poring over a rubric.

Peer and self-assessment is another form of formative feedback which, when done well, can be particularly effective in motivating students to move forward in their learning (NFER, 2018). When introducing it in the classroom, it is important that teachers and learning support assistants spend some time modelling the process and demonstrating how things like constructive feedback should be given. This will make it easier for students to assess their own work, as they will find it simpler to identify weaknesses in their own work and see how they can make improvements. Black and Wiliam reported gains in the achievement of students who had been involved in peer and self-assessment (Black and Wiliam, 1998; Assessment Reform Group, 1999), so if students are supported and scaffolded in this process, it will help them to reflect on and improve their work.

Finally, the use of data can be effective in improving student outcomes, although too much data can become meaningless and confusing. When test scores are used as part of data-based decision-making, the focus should be on gathering information on student learning across a period of time. Not only can this data be used to track progress, but with summative examinations such as GCSEs or SATs, it can help schools to adapt, so the teaching in areas where groups of students didn't do as well in the exams can be re-evaluated and strengthened.

Focus group findings

A few of the NQTs in the focus group felt that assessment pitfalls, and how to avoid them, were only discussed in broad terms by their mentor, but that, thankfully, they received help and support on what not to do from other colleagues in their department, such as recently qualified teachers. One interviewee remembered observing teachers assessing prior knowledge and understanding during lessons in their training year, but they weren't given much support on how to actually do this during their NQT year. However, another NQT spoke glowingly about the support they were offered: 'We did a lot of moderating and marked things together as well as went through walk-through lessons before I taught them; my mentor was really amazing at sharing resources and observing me in feedback lessons, and I feel like this is the area I made the most progress in.' They felt that this helped them to mark more regularly and teach more responsively, as the marking took significantly less time than trawling through each student's book. Others recalled that they had worked in groups with more experienced colleagues, and another NQT was given lots of opportunities to team-mark papers and assessments with more expert colleagues and have discussions about how marks had been awarded. As they were part of this process, they spoke about how they felt more empowered to speak out and give their opinions, or even to disagree with marks if they felt they could justify it.

Unfortunately, this openness was not what all early career teachers experienced: one teacher gave an account of a time when they had tried to disagree on a mark that an experienced teacher had given on some moderation of mock exams and was told in front of the rest of the department that they were wrong and that they would do well to trust those who had been doing it longer. After this incident, they felt too intimidated to speak up in similar situations as they felt that they had little to offer.

Another NQT spoke about the fact that they were often given the freedom to do what they initially thought was the right thing to do and given advice later if it was needed. They recalled a Year 8 lesson where they had planned to do an assessment of prior knowledge, which was a short 20 minute test about the information the students should know from Key Stage 2. Their mentor advised that sometimes these types of assessments do not work, as you can only adapt your teaching once you have marked them. But they added that if the mentee wanted to try out this method they could. They said: 'I went forward and tried it anyway and found that she was right – my planning for the rest of that lesson was wasted as the students didn't remember all the information from Key Stage 2 and this was evident in the tests I had given them. Moving forward we decided to use the time instead to revisit the content for 20 minutes, which would be a better use of time.' The questioning they learned during that time to assess students' prior understanding has stayed with them and still sits at the centre of their lessons.

Many participants felt that they had learned a lot about the various forms of assessment through lesson observations and the subsequent feedback. One early career teacher was advised to improve their targeted questioning when they were employing formative assessment, and their mentor organised a three week mini course to work on that skill. They also had focused lesson observations during which their explanations of key concepts were scrutinised. It was noted that they were rushing through content, so the mentor then spent an hour each week over the next fortnight going through strategies to break them down further.

The guidance received about how to provide high quality feedback and what this looks like was more detailed, but mostly seemed to be aimed at matching school approaches and policies. Mentors wanted new teachers to convey a positive and encouraging message, but not to praise excessively when something remarkable had been done. This seemed strange to one NQT, but it seemed to work for their context, so they took their mentor's advice. Another teacher's mentor was fantastic at helping them with assessment and feedback. They would encourage them to join in with department moderation with their own books and also encourage them to check their assessment marking with more experienced teachers if they were unsure. In the first few weeks, their mentor would also sit with them when marking books and assessments or would ask them to bring a few books to the mentor meetings to quality assure their feedback. They also gave them tips on how to mark effectively – starting with pupil premium books and only marking relevant sections. They would also show their mentor lesson plans or the outline of lesson plans during the meetings. They then moved on to outlining a week's worth of lessons, which the NQT felt was very effective in helping them to see the bigger picture of what they wanted the students to be achieving. They liked that this was done in such a way that the mentor didn't control their lesson plans, just guided and advised, so the mentee could learn and improve.

One of the things that all of the NQTs in the focus group struggled with was how to make the marking workload more manageable. Most were advised to try and keep on top of their marking and to ask for help if they were struggling. To help with this, some schools held weekly sessions where books could be shared; this provided opportunities for teachers to share advice and pick up tips from more experienced colleagues. Another NQT in the study realised that they were struggling because they were taking too long to mark individual pieces of work. To help them, their mentor went through the marking policy and suggested practical ways that the new teacher could apply it more efficiently. They regularly marked pieces of work together and the mentor would always seem happy to moderate one or two assignments. If the NQT was way off in the marking, the mentor would explain why they would have awarded a different mark, but they would also listen to the new teacher if they wanted to justify the mark they had given. The NQT added: 'It always felt like we were supporting one another, rather than my marking being interrogated.' Another participant spoke about how their mentor had suggested that they mark for literacy (highlighting spelling, punctuation and grammar mistakes in students' books) during the lesson. In this way, they had less marking to do outside of lessons and were more able to keep on top of workload demands.

How can I help my mentee meet this standard?

To begin with, you need to be able to spend some time with the NQT looking at medium-term plans in your department and guiding them to identify where the opportunities for formative assessment would fall. A worthwhile exercise would be to have some lesson objectives written down in the middle of a page and to ask the mentee to produce some ideas about formative assessment types and examples they could use which are linked to the objective and would show student understanding. These could then be mapped across a scheme of work so that, taken together, they could show patterns of student performance and guide what would be taught later on. Several different types of tasks work well for formative or summative assessment and some of these are detailed in Table 6.1.

Table 6.1. Task ideas for formative and summative assessment

	Formative assessment	Summative assessment
Informal	Questioning Feedback Peer assessment Self-assessment	Essays in uncontrolled conditions Portfolios Coursework Teacher assessment
Formal	Further analysis or tests Exams Essays Target setting	Tests Exams Essays in controlled conditions

For summative assessments, it is important that your NQT has access to the exam board's website, so they can retrieve the official, externally validated materials to use in controlled conditions in class. It is surprising how many teachers do not have access to these sample papers. When I moved schools after seven years in the profession, I changed exam boards. On arrival, I asked a middle leader in my department if I could have access to the exam board's secure website and copies of the specification, and I was told that as a classroom teacher I didn't need to know that information! Not only is this bizarre, it is also extremely limiting; there is a vast amount of knowledge, guidance and materials on exam board websites and every teacher should be allowed to read them. Your exams officer should be able to grant you access and send you a username and password.

To help the new teacher adapt their teaching and identify the gaps in their students' learning, it is important that they possess a number of strategies for checking prior knowledge. There are many ways to do this – from using multiple-choice questionnaires, where some of the options contain common misconceptions, to setting a quick-six quiz as a starter activity. Another good idea is to produce an encyclopaedia entry about a topic with four or five content errors and ask the students to find them or compare the entry with a credible source. Not only will this help with critical analysis skills, but it may also correct any misunderstandings and show the teacher which areas need more work. Another option is to use self-assessment tools such as LINK grids (see Figure 6.2), where students note down everything they know about a topic, which can then be discussed as a class and any gaps filled in. At the end of the lesson, the students can finish by writing down what they know in the 'K' box and then rip it off and hand it to the teacher on their way out. This can then be used to inform future planning.

L	I	N	K
(List everything you know)	(Inquire about what you want to know)	(Now we are going to take notes)	(What do you know now?)

Figure 6.2. Example of a link grid template

Using peers and collaborative knowledge sharing can also be a great way of assessing prior knowledge. At the start of the lesson, the students could complete a mind map on a topic chosen by the teacher, and then brainstorm on their own what they already know about it. Next, they can discuss their ideas with a peer and add any new knowledge to the mind map in a different colour pen (see Figure 6.3). Once this has been done, the class can finally discuss what they know collectively as a group and the teacher can add all of that knowledge to a class mind map. This information can then be added to the students' diagrams in another colour, while the teacher circulates the room and gives feedback or chats about any misconceptions. This exercise can then inform the next phase of the learning.

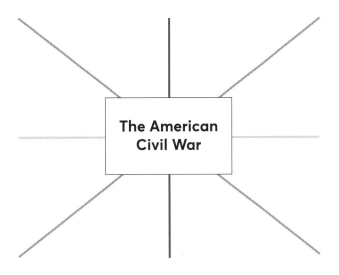

The American Civil War

Figure 6.3. Mind map activity

We considered questioning in Chapter 4, but it is also a vital tool when assessing understanding through formative assessment. Tasks and questions need to be carefully structured so the students are prompted to elaborate on their answers and, in turn, teachers are able to check that the answer they give stems from secure understanding and knowledge. In lessons, different questioning techniques serve different purposes and they all have a place when interrogating students' knowledge. When checking your mentee's planning, have a conversation about what types of questions they will employ and what kind of information about prior understanding they will be able to elicit from them. Table 6.2 categorises the different question types and why they are used, with some useful examples of question stems that your NQT can adapt.

Table 6.2. Question examples (adapted from Fisher and Frey, 2010)

Question type	Purpose	Examples
Elicitation	To unearth misconceptions and check for factual knowledge.	• Who …? • What …? • When …? • Where …? • Why …? • How …?
Elaboration	To extend the length and the complexity of the response.	• Can you tell me more about that? • What other information do I need to know?
Clarification	To gain further details.	• Can you show me where you found that information? • Why did you choose that answer?
Divergent	To discover how the student uses their existing knowledge to formulate new understanding.	• What if the Allied Forces had not defeated the Nazis in the Second World War – what would the world be like today?

Question type	Purpose	Examples
		• Do snakes and worms have anything in common?
Heuristic	To determine the learner's ability to problem-solve.	• How would you work out the meaning of this word? • If I was searching for information about Picasso, where would I look in this book?
Inventive	To stimulate imaginative thought.	• What advice would you give to Winston Churchill during the Second World War? • How might George feel when Lennie gets into the fight?

When guiding your mentee on how to provide high quality feedback, it is necessary for you to possess a solid understanding of the different types of written feedback and the evidence behind what types of written marking work best. An excellent start to building this knowledge would be to read the EEF's *A Marked Improvement?* (Elliott et al. 2016). It provides recommendations on the types of feedback that really help students to make progress and which can be built into any teacher's routines. Clearly, the school's marking policy needs to be adhered to, but luckily many schools are now realising that expecting teachers to provide excessive amounts of written feedback is unsustainable and has little impact.

In Ross Morrison McGill's *Mark. Plan. Teach* (2017), there are some amazing ideas for how to make formative assessment more productive and useful. The book is well worth a read, but if time is tight, McGill has also published PDF versions of some of his strategies on his blog, @TeacherToolkit.[1] One of the feedback types he advocates is verbal feedback, which he states must be used to 'motivate, manage confidence and provide the right pitch of feedback' (McGill, 2018). You could role play how to do this with your new teacher by showing them how to start with a specific compliment about a student's work and then giving a measurable target for something they can improve. For example, 'I really like the way you have used those violent verbs to show the power of the wind. How about adding a metaphor to compare it to something

---

1   See https://www.teachertoolkit.co.uk/2018/11/05/mark-plan-teach-teaching-and-learning.

dangerous and deadly?' This can then be checked up on later to see whether the student has actioned the advice.

Some websites sell verbal feedback stamps or stickers. These can be useful if used well; if not, they become superficial and for the benefit of middle leaders doing book scrutinies. I have previously used verbal feedback stamps and I like them: I speak to every student while I am circulating the room, and once I have given them some feedback I stamp their book. They have been trained to bullet point the feedback I give them next to the stamp, which they then action and tick after completing.

As explained in earlier chapters, it is essential that students know what good perfor-mance looks like, particularly when they are completing peer or self-assessment. A good way of doing this is to use examples of work from previous students, so it would be worth gathering these from your own classes and from colleagues in the depart-ment to share with your mentee. It may be tempting for the early career practitioner to write their own model answers, but this can be less effective for the students because it may be of a standard that they think is unattainable. This is fine when live modelling, as the teacher can explain how they are formulating their answer, but without this metacognitive commentary, the exemplar can lose its power as the stu-dents are unsure how to get to the finished product. With an example by a former student, however, the teacher can model to the class the type of constructive, specific feedback they might give or provide the student assessors with a list of questions to consider. It is important that opportunities for peer and self-assessment are well structured so students can become accustomed to the process before they are asked to evaluate and comment on the work of their classmates. TAs can also help here, as they can act as a critical buddy or support while the assessments are taking place.

Other forms of feedback, such as whole class feedback sheets or class marking codes, can be an efficient way of approaching marking and giving feedback. Not only are they effective but they save teachers a lot of time. Some schools have specific pro formas for whole class marking that they require all teachers to use and departments may have subject specific marking codes. In a book I wrote on teacher wellbeing aimed at more experienced teachers, I have included exemplars of both of these types of pro forma that your NQT could adapt and trial if the school does not have their own (Hughes, 2020). Comparative judgement could also be trialled in one of your meetings, where you both look at pairs of assessments and have a discussion about which one is better and why. This will make your NQT more confident in their own judgements and more confident about the assessment criteria. Daisy Christodoulou runs regular webinars on this process which it would be very beneficial for your NQT, and even you, to attend.[2]

---

2   See https://www.nomoremarking.com/events2.

Finally, for a full understanding of assessment for learning, it is worth reading the classic *Inside the Black Box* (Black and Wiliam, 1998), which offers a comprehensive research review and will enable your mentee to understand how assessment can be used to underpin teaching and learning.

Chapter 6: Summary

Identify goal:
To make accurate and productive use of assessment which provides teachers with information about students' understanding and needs and to inform decisions about planning. To also use a range of feedback strategies which support students to monitor and regulate their own learning.

Evaluate and reflect on the standard:
- Does the NQT now have an understanding about the ways that lessons can be adapted to meet the needs of all learners?
- Ask them to rate their confidence and identify areas where they need more support.
- Create an action plan for further reading and next steps to develop their skills.

Standard 6 –
Make accurate and productive use of assessment

Apply the learning:
- Provide the NQT with some lesson objectives or intentions and ask them to link them with formative assessment tasks to trial that week. These can then be reflected on in next week's meeting.
- Experiment with some of the activities detailed in this chapter to assess students' prior knowledge and compare the impact together.
- Each half term, ask the NQT to trial using some of the formative assessment tips on Ross Morrison McGill's @TeacherToolkit blog with the same class.
- Work closely with the NQT and TAs to ensure they are clear about what excellence looks like, so they can provide effective verbal feedback.
- Encourage the NQT to try different ways of feeding back, such as whole class marking or class codes.

Come up with a plan:

- Ask your NQT to read *Inside the Black Box* (Black and Wiliam, 1998) for an understanding of assessment for learning.
- Give your mentee access to the department's medium-term plans and ask them to identify places that would make good opportunities to do some formative assessment. Get them to identify which types would work well and explain why.
- Ask the exams officer for a username and password for the exam board's secure area for the new teacher and show them how to navigate the site.
- Buy a verbal feedback stamp or stickers (if using) to record verbal targets and prompt improvements to students' work.
- Begin to collect good examples of work to model how students can use peer and self-assessment.

Learn together:

- Both bring some planning to a meeting and use the question example table (Table 6.2) to discuss where you would ask a particular type of question and why.
- Read Elliott et al. (2016) together and start to trial the strategies to produce a bank of resources that the department can use.
- Independently read McGill's *Mark. Plan. Teach* (2017) and come together to discuss the strategies on formative assessment.
- Collaboratively plan a lesson where students will be taught how to peer and self-assess properly and together produce resources to scaffold this.
- Both sign up to attend a comparative judgement webinar and try to assess some student work using the skills learned.

Chapter 7

Manage behaviour effectively

Managing behaviour (Standard 7 – Manage behaviour effectively)	
Learn that ...	**Learn how to ...**
1. Establishing and reinforcing routines, including through positive reinforcement, can help to create an effective learning environment. 2. A predictable and secure environment benefits all pupils, but is particularly valuable for pupils with special educational needs. 3. The ability to self-regulate one's emotions affects pupils' ability to learn, success in school and future lives. 4. Teachers can influence pupils' resilience and beliefs about their ability to succeed by ensuring all pupils have the opportunity to experience meaningful success. 5. Building effective relationships is easier when pupils believe that their feelings will be considered and understood.	**Develop a positive, predictable and safe environment for pupils, by:** • *Establishing a supportive and inclusive environment with a predictable system of reward and sanction in the classroom.* • *Working alongside colleagues as part of a wider system of behaviour management (e.g. recognising responsibilities and understanding the right to assistance and training from senior colleagues).* • *Giving manageable, specific and sequential instructions.* • *Checking pupils' understanding of instructions before a task begins.* • *Using consistent language and non-verbal signals for common classroom directions.* • *Using early and least intrusive interventions as an initial response to low level disruption.*

Managing behaviour (Standard 7 – Manage behaviour effectively)

Learn that ...	Learn how to ...
6. Pupils are motivated by intrinsic factors (related to their identity and values) and extrinsic factors (related to reward). 7. Pupils' investment in learning is also driven by their prior experiences and perceptions of success and failure.	• *Responding quickly to any behaviour or bullying that threatens emotional safety.* **Establish effective routines and expectations, by:** • *Creating and explicitly teaching routines in line with the school ethos that maximise time for learning (e.g. setting and reinforcing expectations about key transition points).* • *Practising routines at the beginning of the school year.* • *Reinforcing routines (e.g. by articulating the link between time on task and success).* **Build trusting relationships, by:** • *Liaising with parents, carers and colleagues to better understand pupils' individual circumstances and how they can be supported to meet high academic and behavioural expectations.* • *Responding consistently to pupil behaviour.* **Motivate pupils, by:** • *Supporting pupils to master challenging content, which builds towards long-term goals.* • *Providing opportunities for pupils to articulate their long-term goals and helping them to see how these are related to their success in school.*

Managing behaviour (Standard 7 – Manage behaviour effectively)	
Learn that ...	**Learn how to ...**
	• *Helping pupils to journey from needing extrinsic motivation to being motivated to work intrinsically.*

Notes

Learn that ... statements are informed by the best available educational research.

Learn how to ... statements are drawn from the wider evidence base including both academic research and additional guidance from expert practitioners.

Why is this standard important? What does the research say?

Behaviour is always a hot topic in schools as it can literally make or break a career. Three-quarters of teachers say that they frequently have to deal with disruptive behaviour and many have considered quitting the classroom altogether, with almost two-thirds of teachers considering leaving the profession due to it (Williams, 2018). During your two years as a mentor of an early career teacher, there are undoubtedly going to be times when they will need your support with behaviour, so it is helpful to explore what the research says about behaviour management in order to build a solid foundation of strategies. Clearly, teaching in a school and managing so many young people's behaviours is never going to be easy, but the school culture is instrumental in shaping children's behaviour, so it is important to get it right (Chapman et al., 2011).

Establishing routines and using positive reinforcement can create a productive learning environment, as the students know the rules and consequences for their behaviour; it is predictable and inclusive because the rules are the same for everybody. Learning environments are crucial because there is a relationship between a person's behaviour and their surroundings (Kern and Clemens, 2007). There is a rapidly growing body of evidence which suggests that focusing on purely punitive responses may not be sufficiently comprehensive (Newcomer and Lewis, 2004) and that, instead, the environmental pressures which are causing the disruptive behaviours should be altered (Kern et al., 2006). Also, rather than concentrating on punishments, if consistent language and expectations are used, you can try to intervene before the problematic behaviour takes place. This will involve analysing information about what situations might cause undesirable behaviour and changing the environment in some way. This may include the establishment of a positive, motivating, orderly and predictable classroom which promotes appropriate student behaviour; as a result, students are clear what is expected of them and know that this is the right way to behave (Sugai et al., 2002). These antecedent strategies can take the form of whole class or individualised interventions, and will be discussed in more detail later in this chapter.

It is important that within this positive, predictable classroom environment, students feel safe and accepted. There is evidence that there is a strong correlation between students behaving well and feeling a sense of connectedness and attachment to their school (Libbey, 2004). According to Goodenow (1993: 80), 'the extent to which students feel personally accepted, respected, included and supported by others in the school social environment' is of massive importance. Building trusting relationships with students so they want to behave – because they believe their feelings will be considered and understood – is the bedrock of achieving this sense of school connectedness. In some respects, the relationship between students and teachers can be seen as an extension of attachment theory, which usually refers to the bonding that is developed between parents and infants. However, research has shown that bonding with other adults, such as teachers, also has worthwhile effects on resilience (Werner and Smith, 1992). Therefore, many of the behaviour interventions that seem to have the most success include a focus on the positive reinforcement of social skills and developing relationships with teachers and peers (Patton et al., 2003). This suggests that strong and secure emotional connections are an important base for children's social development (Battistich et al. 2000, 2004).

Positive relationships and creating a culture where all think it is positive and acceptable to work hard and achieve can improve behaviour; research investigating interventions which mitigate negative stereotypes, such as 'it's not cool to study', revealed that academic performance soared after value affirmation interventions (Taylor and Walton, 2011). Furthermore, in some research conducted by the Institute of Education Sciences (Epstein et al., 2008), it was revealed that an estimated one-third of students fail to learn due to behaviour in the classroom which interferes with their ability to fully focus and engage in instructional activities. They suggested five approaches to deal with these barriers to learning which aim to improve classroom environments and reduce disruptive or distracting behaviours (see Table 7.1).

Table 7.1. Strategies to reduce behaviour problems
(adapted from Epstein et al., 2008)

1.	2.	3.	4.	5.
Identify the specifics of the problem behaviour and the conditions that prompt and reinforce it.	Modify the classroom learning environment to decrease problem behaviour.	Teach and reinforce new skills to increase appropriate behaviour and preserve a positive classroom climate.	Draw on relationships with professional colleagues and students' families for continued guidance and support.	Assess whether schoolwide behaviour problems warrant adopting schoolwide strategies or programs and, if so, implement ones shown to reduce negative interactions and foster positive interactions.

These strategies are a very useful starting point for establishing a purposeful environment at the start of the year. The 'How can I help my mentee meet this standard?' section will explore ideas for using them practically in the classroom.

In Willingham's *Why Don't Students Like School?* (2009: 11), he discusses how important teachers can be to the success of students:

Ask ten people you know, 'Who was the most important teacher in your life?' I've asked dozens of people this question and have noticed two interesting things. First, most people have a ready answer. Second, the reason that one teacher made a strong impression is almost always emotional. The reasons are never things like 'She taught me a lot of math.' People say things like 'She made me believe in myself' or 'She taught me to love knowledge.'

Praise and creating a secure environment are both so important, and is particularly valuable to those students who have special educational needs. Both parents and teachers are at the heart of ensuring that learners with special educational needs receive a good quality of learning, so it is vital that teachers draw on the best available evidence to plan and teach appropriately and inclusively (Mitchell, 2014). In 2017, the Department for Education released a guidance report on how best to support students with special educational needs in lessons (Carroll et al., 2017), which included advice on successfully managing behaviour. To support attention and on-task behaviour, the report explores a number of different interventions, including: self-management and self-regulation, mindfulness training, student logs, homework and organisational skills. The report is filled with ideas for interventions for many different types of special educational need, but in my view, some focus is needed here on strategies to use with children who have social, emotional and mental health (SEMH) issues, such as attention deficit hyperactivity disorder (ADHD), as these can sometimes be the most challenging to deal with in the classroom. Although many schools run on a system of consequence-based behaviour interventions, research has found that these strategies alone are not effective with students with ADHD, and professionals need to look beyond the child to find out what the causes of the behaviours are and eliminate those (Humphrey and Brooks, 2006).

In addition, it is vital that a school-wide approach to behaviour is consistent so that students with SEMH issues can achieve and develop a healthy sense of self. Research from DuPaul and Weyandt (2006), concludes that the most effective way to help these students learn is through a multimodal approach where both proactive and reactive classroom interventions are used. Proactive treatments (such as peer tutoring or choice-making) and reactive treatments (like token reinforcement, self-management interventions and changing the environmental conditions) have achieved the most success. The range of strategies discussed in Carroll et al.'s (2017) guidance is vast and incredibly thorough and useful; it is an important tool for teachers and would be worth exploring with your mentee.

When managing behaviour it is not just the students' behaviour that needs to change; sometimes teachers are the real catalyst, so they need to exemplify the boundaries and behavioural expectations themselves rather than flood students with thousands of rules. Paul Dix's work focuses on ideas based around restorative practice, and his book, *When the Adults Change, Everything Changes* (2017), is full of advice on building a whole school ethos of kindness, empathy and understanding. He stresses the importance of consistency by stating: 'if you don't shape a visible positive consistency between the adults, then you open the door to them breeding their own negative consistency' (Dix, 2017: 5). He concludes that focusing on changing the behaviour of teachers and other adults in a school is the only sensible approach, as we should be in control of our own emotions before we attempt to control the emotions of our students. This is a skill. There will be times when your NQT may lose their temper or get upset and have to take a breather to avoid dealing with challenging behaviour in a damaging way. They may need your help to learn to self-regulate their emotions.

Self-regulation for students was mentioned briefly earlier on in this literature review, but its importance in the development of successful learners means that it is worth analysing in more detail. Self-regulation can be defined in terms of temperament and effort of attention (Valiente et al., 2008), emotional wellbeing and forming positive relationships (Mashburn and Pianta, 2006), the ability to be resilient (Mischel et al., 1989), or executive functions like being able to organise themselves or not break rules and work on tasks that are goal related (McClelland et al., 2007). Studies have revealed that self-regulation meaningfully predicts school achievement, and Ursache et al. (2012) have created a self-regulation model which links emotion with cognition, and state that executive function is important for fostering interest, engagement and motivation. Zimmerman (2000) and Pintrich and Zusho (2001) concur and state that the best self-regulated learning occurs when students are motivated to want to achieve and when they direct their efforts towards activities which are employed towards the attainment of goals. These challenges provide a means for self-regulated learning to occur (Hadwin et al., 2010). There are ways that teachers can help students to become more self-regulated, which mostly involve empowering them to plan, search, learn and reflect. The model by Nussbaumer et al. (2014) (Figure 7.1) shows how teachers have more of a facilitating role in this process and that they almost need to 'train' students to be more self-regulatory. Specific and practical ways of doing this will be explored in the 'How can I help my mentee meet this standard?' section of this chapter.

The ability to self-regulate emotions is inextricably tied up in how successfully students can learn – particularly their resilience and how much they believe they are capable of success. Aside from having a predictable classroom structure with clear routines, teachers can influence students' beliefs about their own abilities by providing opportunities for them to experience meaningful success. In Chapter 3, we discussed Rosenshine's (2012) suggestion that scaffolds should only be taken away when students achieve a success rate of 80% when applying previously taught material. Yet resilience is not just about academic success; it is also about students knowing that it is okay to fail and that failing is part of the learning process. There is also a significant emotional component to resilience, which means that they need loving support to build their own self-confidence, so they can have faith in themselves and their world view.

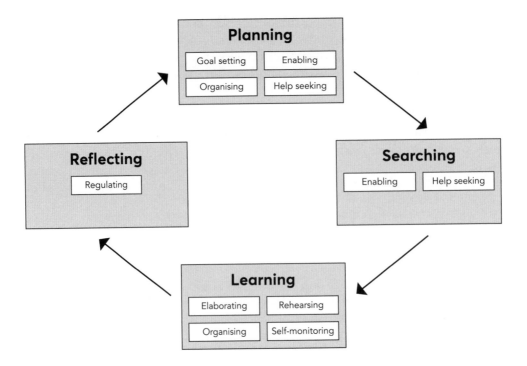

Figure 7.1. How teachers can help students to become self-regulated learners (adapted from Nussbaumer et al., 2014)

Some research has pointed towards the success of using models such as 'I have, I am, I can' to build more resilience. The model refers to the three sources of resilience that children can draw from (see Table 7.2); if one of the resilience sources is lacking, teachers can develop this strand with them. For example, a student might not feel they have people around them they can trust, so the teacher needs to build a trusting relationship and ensure that they feel this relationship is consistent, predictable and secure. If one of the roles of schooling is to equip students for life as an adult, then the importance of resilience cannot be underestimated. We all experience adverse situations at some stage, so these lessons learned as a child will equip them with the tools to triumph over possible future trauma and achieve success.

Table 7.2. The 'I have, I am, I can' resilience model (adapted from Grotberg, 1995)

I have ...	I am ...	I can ...
People who I trust who will love me no matter what.	Someone who people can like and love.	Speak to others about things that bother or frighten me.
People who protect me by setting limits for me.	Happy to do good things for others and show if I am concerned or worried.	Work to find solutions to problems that I may face.
People who model and show me the right way to do things.	Respectful of others and myself.	Control myself and stop myself from doing something which is wrong or dangerous.
People who want me to be more independent and learn things on my own.	Willing to accept responsibility for the things I do.	Realise when it is a good time to chat to someone or take action about something.
People who will help when I am ill or in danger or need to learn.	Secure in the knowledge that things will be okay.	Seek out and find someone to help me when needed.

Motivation is strongly correlated with resilience and the ability to self-regulate our emotions. Ford (1992) asserts that motivation is made up of an interrelated mixture of goals, emotions and personal beliefs, which he formulates in this equation:

Motivation = goals × emotions × personal agency beliefs

Our goals are important because much of our behaviour is governed by them: we want to achieve positive desired outcomes and avoid negative undesired outcomes. However, Ford makes a distinction between task and ability focused goals, and states that learners tend to prefer one type of goal over another. As teachers, therefore, we need to ascertain which one will motivate our students. Task focused goals are more about mastering tasks and learning for intrinsic reasons, such as improvement and believing that we get better with effort. Students who are motivated by this type of goal may be more likely to engage in making connections between previously learned and new content and show greater persistence when faced with obstacles. In contrast, those who are more motivated by ability focused goals prefer to gain favourable judgements or outperform others, so they can avoid failure. Sometimes, these students can have more of a fixed mindset as they may believe that ability and intelligence is inherited and permanent, so they may avoid challenge due to their fear of appearing to fail. This may also result in them exhibiting negative behaviours when they are confronted by obstacles. Consequently, educators should help their students to become more task focused so they are able to regulate their emotions, become more resilient and, ultimately, become more motivated.

Dix (2017) advocates restorative conversations between teachers and students to motivate them to repair relationships which may have become strained. If done well, he claims that restorative conversations (sometimes called restorative justice) can totally transform behaviour and not only repair but also improve relationships. To ensure that these meetings are successful, they must be run by someone independent and involve the following six questions:

1. What has happened?
2. What were you thinking at the time (class teacher and child)?
3. Who has been affected by the actions?
4. How have they been affected?
5. What needs to be done now to make things right?
6. How can we do things differently in the future?

When done right, restorative conversations can repair relationships and make a huge difference; however, when handled badly, they can make life even more difficult for teachers as they can feel attacked and blamed, making the situation seem even more impossible. There is no doubt, though, that relationships are a major motivation in whether students choose to behave in lessons.

Another motivator is parents; as a predictor of academic achievement and motivation, the National PTA (2000) claim that the extent to which families encourage learning at home and involve themselves in their child's education can determine a student's level of academic success. Having support at home and help when needed to complete assignments and homework can instil a lifelong love of learning, so when teachers focus on engaging parents, they often see a profound change in the motivation levels of students (Waterford, 2018). Therefore, encouraging and promoting parental engagement is one of the best ways to inspire and drive students to want to succeed and create a culture of aspiration and motivation in the classroom.

Focus group findings

The early career teachers in the focus group felt that behaviour was one of the most regular discussion points in their weekly mentor meetings, and that this made them feel supported and gave them that anchored time for reflection which is so necessary. One NQT felt that mentors had a significant role in developing a new teacher's confidence, and also that mentors should keep a record of what was discussed and should be put in place, so that these strategies could be followed up on and reflected on later. Another participant felt that they were struggling with self-confidence and couldn't see the positive impact they were having on their students. Their mentor suggested asking the class to write down on a sticky note something the teacher had taught them, what this meant to them and what they enjoyed about their classes. This really improved the teacher's confidence: 'By mentors doing small but tangible and hugely impactful actions like that, it can improve the mentee's relationship with their class as well as the relationship with their own identity and self-doubt.'

Other comments focused on the trust that needs to exist between mentor and NQT to enable them to grow. Part of this is knowledge about when to intervene and when to let new teachers face the challenge and learn from it. A teacher in the group spoke about how they felt their mentor had inadvertently undermined them on a fairly regular basis. They said, 'There were times when I was dealing with a situation and they would just burst in and kind of take over … They meant well but I didn't feel like I was learning how to deal with challenging situations because they were always swooping in to rescue me. It was very frustrating.' Clearly, there needs to be a distinction between supporting and taking over, and a discussion with your NQT will ascertain where those boundaries lie.

The best mentors seemed to stress how important it was to observe behaviour management strategies in action in different lessons and classrooms and talk to other members of staff about what works and what doesn't. They also supported the new teachers with implementing the school's behaviour policy as consistently as possible and by instilling the belief that using 'on call' systems or sanctions does not mean that you are incapable or less of a teacher. In one school, a participant divulged that half termly data on how many 'on calls' each teacher has used is circulated to the whole staff via email. This made them feel that asking for support was shameful and that they needed to ask for less to avoid facing embarrassment and judgement from their colleagues. Not only is this degrading, but it is also extremely unhelpful as it makes new teachers afraid to ask for help.

There is no doubt that being consistent can be tough. One teacher said, 'After a long hard day and when you've marked 30 books, it's easy to forget that you promised you'd phone home for excellent effort or that you need to add that behaviour point. But if you make a habit of following though, the students trust that you mean what you say.' Managing behaviour doesn't just mean recording negative incidents; it also means celebrating positive behaviours, hard work and consistent effort. An early career teacher spoke glowingly about the way their school had encouraged them to do this by furnishing them with postcards and prizes to give to the class when they behaved well. Another teacher recounted that their mentor had allowed them to listen in on positive telephone conversations they had with parents, so they could model the same kind of dialogue themselves.

One mentor spent a lot of time discussing how to develop a professional pastoral relationship with students and stressed that students aren't looking for somebody who gives 'whizz-bang lessons all the time – you're not an entertainer, you're a teacher'. They need someone who is consistent in their expectations and standards, and challenge is the best way to instil this. They added, 'Success comes before motivation – if a student feels like they can be consistently successful in some way in your lesson, the motivation will follow.' Another mentor had noticed that the mentee was getting 'too pally' with the kids, resulting in the lines between teacher and student becoming blurred. They gave them some advice on how to avoid this, which really helped them to strike the correct balance.

How can I help my mentee meet this standard?

The key to helping your mentee establish a positive, inclusive and safe environment for students is predictability and consistency. Students need to feel supported and to know what systems of rewards and sanctions are used in the school. This means working together with other colleagues in your department and across the school to manage behaviour properly, and also to make it clear to the new teacher that you are there to help, if needed, and so are senior colleagues. As an NQT, I had a mentor who made me believe that she never had behaviour issues in her lessons and that using 'on call' systems was somehow a weakness. This made me feel like a failure when trying to manage disruptive behaviour, so instead of asking for help when I needed it, I suffered alone and felt quite helpless. It was only after I had observed my mentor teaching that I realised that behaviour was terrible in her lessons – but she just ignored it! You can help your NQT with behaviour management by enabling them to observe as many different teachers and classes as possible, so they can see how experienced practitioners are employing consistent language and non-verbal signals to stop disruptive behaviour in its tracks. These observations could then inform a professional discussion on how the new teacher could implement some of these in their own classroom.

While asking for help should be encouraged, supporting early career teachers to develop low-key strategies as initial interventions for negative behaviour can also aid them in taking control of the learning in their lessons. As discussed, setting the stage with consistent rules and language is a good start, but modifying the curriculum and the way that teachers give instructions can also help to reduce the amount of disruptive behaviour. One of the reasons that negative behaviour may occur is because students feel bored and disengaged or do not understand the task. Therefore, it is important to model how new teachers can give manageable, specific and sequential instructions. Perhaps you could invite the teacher to observe your own lesson with a focus on the following elements: how long and specific instructions are, the pacing of instructions, how instructions are modified when misunderstanding occurs, and whether there are multiple modes of instruction. The NQT could then provide you with feedback and you could work collaboratively on ways to improve this aspect of delivering instructions. It may also be beneficial to conduct some student voice using a clarity of instruction pro forma (Table 7.3) after a lesson to see what the students feel could be improved. The evaluation form could also be used in role playing activities between yourself and the new teacher.

Table 7.3. Student voice clarity of instruction pro forma

Question	Response
Which instructions were difficult to follow? Why?	
What vocabulary did you not understand? Did your teacher explain it?	

Question	Response					
Did you understand the lesson objectives?						
What would have helped you understand the instructions more?						
Which parts of the lesson grabbed your attention? Why?						
How would you rate the clarity of your teacher's instructions overall?	**Very clear**					**Very confusing**
	5	4	3	2	1	0

Instructions need to be well sequenced so they will advance the students' understanding of content with a set of steps that will help learning to occur. Sequencing is important because if a student is asked to complete a task and they do not have the necessary knowledge and skills, they will be unable to do so. When planning instructional design and sequencing, a good beginning point is to identify the learning goal and think about whether the lesson sequencing is leading students towards this goal. It may be worth reviewing a sample of the NQT's lesson plans together using some of the following questions to structure the discussion:

- Is it linear? Are the instructions designed along a continuum where activities at the beginning of the lesson are less cognitively demanding than the tasks at the end?

- Is the instructional design hierarchical? Is each phase more difficult than the one that came before so that students are scaffolded to complete challenges? Is the teacher gradually allowing students more time to complete tasks independently?

- Are there opportunities for students to experience success? This will increase positive feelings, motivation and investment in the lesson.

If the lesson plans they bring to the meeting don't show that these considerations have been taken into account, you may want to adapt them and plan a lesson together which focuses on providing instructions that help students to stay engaged and behave positively.

As mentioned earlier in the chapter, there has been some promising research on the success of antecedent strategies which seek to prevent problematic behaviour before it occurs. Kern and Clemens (2007) highlight some strategies that educators can use to do this (Table 7.4). Many of these strategies include communicating and reinforcing routines and matching material to the instructional level, so these strategies can also be considered in the conversations about lesson planning too.

Table 7.4. Antecedent strategies for managing disruptive behaviour (adapted from Kern and Clemens, 2007)

Class strategies	Individual student strategies
Clear classroom rules and expectations. Predictable environment. Praise for good behaviour. Challenging but accessible material. Appropriate classroom layout. Active learning opportunities. Effective instructions. Scaffolding. Well-paced instructions. Opportunities to choose tasks. Appeal to interests.	Challenging but accessible material. Models of varying degrees of success. Appeal to interests. Opportunities to choose tasks. Give students some scheduled attention to reduce attention-seeking behaviour. Clear and predictable schedules.

Another model you may both want to use for reflection on a particularly challenging class is the one produced by Epstein et al. (2008) which was discussed in the research section earlier in this chapter (see Table 7.1). You could provide your mentee with a blank table using strategies suggested in the report and together come up with ideas the teacher could try (see Table 7.5 for a completed version). No matter how long people have been teaching, they will always come across challenging classes, students and situations – it is important that the new teacher realises this – so you could also fill in the table yourself.

Table 7.5. Table of strategies (adapted from Epstein et al., 2008)

Identify the specifics of the problem behaviour and the conditions that prompt and reinforce it.	Modify the classroom learning environment to decrease problem behaviour.
Student keeps displaying disruptive behaviour when the class does independent work and tries to distract others by throwing things or making loud noises. The rest of the class seem to think it's funny and laugh at them, which just makes them do it more.	The student sits near the back of the room, close to some other students who have the potential to be demotivated and silly. Instead, the student could be moved closer to the front and seated next to more motivated and engaged students who can act as positive role models. The TA could work more closely with the student when independent work is done in case they are disengaging because they find it more difficult.

Teach and reinforce new skills to increase appropriate behaviour and preserve a positive classroom climate.	Draw on relationships with professional colleagues and students' families for continued guidance and support.
Reinforce the school and class rules so the student knows that disrupting their peers is not acceptable. Try to instil an atmosphere where it is seen as normal to try hard and achieve, so they don't receive validation from their peers when they act out. Make the student feel empowered to ask for help if needed, and allow them the opportunity to feel academically successful so they build resilience and coping strategies when tasks are more challenging.	Chat to the student's other teachers or prior teachers to see whether they had any particular strategies to keep this student engaged. Check with the SEN team to find out whether there is any data on the student. Use praise to build the student's school connectedness and contact home with positive messages.

As we saw earlier, emotions are inextricably linked with negative behaviour, so many of these problems can be fixed by building trusting relationships with students. This is where communication with the pastoral team becomes so important. In my opinion, primary school teachers have more of a connection with parents and carers as they have the opportunity to meet and converse with them on a daily basis. It is often more difficult for secondary teachers to liaise with parents to better understand their students' individual circumstances. As an English teacher working in a secondary setting, I teach over 150 students a week and other colleagues may teach over 500 students a week. It would be impossible to know the hopes, worries, dreams and feelings of all of them. The head of year or pastoral support, with their unique understanding of the students and their families, can be an invaluable source of information and they will be happy to support your mentee in any way they can.

There may be barriers to challenging students being able to meet your high academic and behavioural expectations, but if you can find out what these are, you can work with parents to help students overcome them. If we go back to the 'I have, I am, I can' model discussed earlier, many strands come back to the idea that students trust their teachers and know they have their best interests at heart. They support students to master more demanding content and relate their long-term goals to being successful in their lessons.

Of course, teachers are not perfect – they are human beings and, sometimes, certain challenging students can be really difficult to reach. I had a very demotivated boy in a top set GCSE class who hated English and was going into the army, so didn't see that he would ever need it or use the skills acquired in the subject in his adult life. To motivate him, I revealed that he needed to at least pass his English GCSE to join the army and then looked at the qualifications and achievements of individuals who had progressed beyond soldier level to more senior positions to demonstrate that 'just passing' would not be enough to compete. It was no longer about grades and scraping through. This student could now visualise himself as an officer in the army – it was now about ambition. Transferring motivation from extrinsic to intrinsic can be difficult, but it comes about through motivating your students, through your relationship with them and through getting to know what their barriers are. Opportunities to do this will occur naturally in lessons; while you are circulating the room you can have a professional dialogue with students during which you can find out about their goals and what motivates them. Parents' evenings are also fantastic for this, and together you can develop a plan for how best to support students to be successful.

The ultimate goal is to help students to become self-regulated learners: they will be able to stay on task because they can use Nussbaumer's strategies of planning, searching, learning and reflecting. But, as alluded to earlier, there are ways that teachers can support students to do this. In the planning stage, it is important that students are given time to plan and are helped to organise themselves when they have set themselves a goal, with the opportunity to seek help if it is needed. When students are learning and completing tasks independently, teachers can help to keep them motivated by encouraging them to elaborate on their work and self-monitor by checking their own work against models of what success looks like. Crucially, the teacher needs to keep the lesson goal relevant so that students can regulate how well they are working towards it. You could reflect on whether students are getting the opportunities to practise these self-regulation strategies in the new teacher's lessons and how well their pedagogy is facilitating this. If they are not, perhaps they can plan a series of lessons where they try to improve this and you can then focus on this in one of your formal observations.

To conclude, behaviour strategies need to be inclusive so that students with special educational needs can also flourish and learn effectively. There are some excellent resources on how best to support these students in the Department for Education's *SEN Support: A Rapid Evidence Assessment* (Carroll et al., 2017). The scope of this book is not wide enough to include the wealth of best practice it contains, and so it would be extremely beneficial if, after looking at their class data and becoming aware of any SEND students, the new teacher could read any relevant sections to find out the best resources for reaching those students. It is vital that every learner is able to experience success in school, and so much of that comes from being able to motivate themselves and self-regulate their emotions, which in turn helps them to build resilience and manage their own behaviour effectively.

Chapter 7: Summary

Identify goal:

To manage behaviour effectively by developing a positive, predictable and safe environment for students and establishing routines through positive reinforcement. Help students to self-regulate their emotions so they can build resilience and believe they can succeed. Do this by building an effective relationship so that students are motivated by intrinsic factors.

Evaluate and reflect on the standard:

- Does the NQT now have an understanding about how to manage behaviour effectively?
- Ask them to rate their confidence and identify areas where they need more support.
- Create an action plan for further reading and next steps to develop their skills.

Standard 7 – Managing behaviour

Apply the learning:

- Ask the new teacher to trial some of the observed behaviour management strategies in their lessons and track to what extent motivation is improved.
- Direct the NQT to ask students to fill in the student voice pro forma on quality of instructions after a lesson (Table 7.3). The completed responses can then be discussed in a mentor meeting, during which you can work on ways to improve the teacher's delivery of instructions.
- After a challenging lesson, use Table 7.5 to analyse the negative behaviour and try to come up with a practical solution.
- Encourage the NQT to liaise with pastoral staff and other colleagues to communicate about the possible causes of barriers to learning.
- Ask them to seize the opportunity to include ways of making their subjects more relevant to their students and explicitly including these in lesson plans.

Come up with a plan:

- Arrange observations across faculties and age ranges for your mentee so they can see how experienced practitioners are employing consistent language and non-verbal signals to stop disruptive behaviour in its tracks.

- Identify a lesson where the NQT could observe your lesson with a focus on: how long and specific instructions are, the pacing of instructions, how instructions are modified when misunderstanding occurs, and whether there are multiple modes of instruction.

- Read Kern and Clemens' (2007) paper on antecedent behaviour strategies and reflect together on how they could be used in challenging situations the NQT has faced.

- After ascertaining the different forms of SEN in your classes, use the Department for Education's SEN report guidance (Carroll et al., 2017) to apply the best strategies.

Learn together:

- Ask the NQT to make notes about what they have observed about other colleagues' behaviour management strategies and bring them to a meeting. Have a practical discussion about how the new teacher could implement some of these in their own classroom.

- After your mentee has observed your lesson with a focus on instructions, ask them to provide you with feedback on their findings and collaboratively discuss ways that instructions could be improved.

- Using some of the NQT's planning, ask them to identify what the learning goals of the lessons are and use the questions on lesson sequencing to explore whether the learning is well sequenced.

Chapter 8

Fulfil wider professional responsibilities

Professional behaviours (Standard 8 – Fulfil wider professional responsibilities)	
Learn that ...	**Learn how to ...**
1. Effective professional development is likely to be sustained over time, involve expert support or coaching and opportunities for collaboration. 2. Reflective practice, supported by feedback from and observation of experienced colleagues, professional debate, and learning from educational research, is also likely to support improvement. 3. Teachers can make valuable contributions to the wider life of the school in a broad range of ways, including by supporting and developing effective professional relationships with colleagues. 4. Building effective relationships with parents, carers and families can improve pupils' motivation, behaviour and academic success.	**Develop as a professional, by:** • *Engaging in professional development focused on developing an area of practice with clear intentions for impact on pupil outcomes, sustained over time with built-in opportunities for practice.* • *Strengthening pedagogical and subject knowledge by participating in wider networks.* • *Seeking challenge, feedback and critique from mentors and other colleagues in an open and trusting working environment.* • *Engaging critically with research and discussing evidence with colleagues.* • *Reflecting on progress made, recognising strengths and weaknesses, and identifying next steps for further improvement.*

Professional behaviours (Standard 8 – Fulfil wider professional responsibilities)	
Learn that ...	**Learn how to ...**
5. Teaching assistants (TAs) can support pupils more effectively when they are prepared for lessons by teachers, and when TAs supplement rather than replace support from teachers. 6. SENCOs, pastoral leaders, careers advisors and other specialist colleagues also have valuable expertise and can ensure that appropriate support is in place for pupils. 7. Engaging in high quality professional development can help teachers improve.	**Build effective working relationships, by:** • *Contributing positively to the wider school culture and developing a feeling of shared responsibility for improving the lives of all pupils within the school.* • *Seeking ways to support individual colleagues and working as part of a team.* • *Communicating with parents and carers proactively and making effective use of parents' evenings to engage parents and carers in their children's schooling.* • *Working closely with the SENCO and other professionals supporting pupils with additional needs, making explicit links between interventions delivered outside of lessons with classroom teaching.* • *Sharing the intended lesson outcomes with teaching assistants ahead of lessons.* • *Ensuring that support provided by teaching assistants in lessons is additional to, rather than a replacement for, support from the teacher.* • *Knowing who to contact with any safeguarding concerns.*

Professional behaviours (Standard 8 – Fulfil wider professional responsibilities)	
Learn that ...	**Learn how to ...**
	Manage workload and wellbeing, by: • *Using and personalising systems and routines to support efficient time and task management.* • *Understanding the right to support (e.g. to deal with misbehaviour).* • *Collaborating with colleagues to share the load of planning and preparation and making use of shared resources (e.g. textbooks).* • *Protecting time for rest and recovery.*

Notes

Learn that ... statements are informed by the best available educational research.

Learn how to ... statements are drawn from the wider evidence base including both academic research and additional guidance from expert practitioners.

Why is this standard important? What does the research say?

Improving professional learning for educators is a crucial step in transforming schools and improving academic achievement. (Wei et al., 2009)

This quote from a report on teacher development sums up how important it is that teachers receive and seek out professional development opportunities. Effective professional development is not only vital to improve student outcomes, but is also a significant part of how teachers reflect on their own practice and refine their pedagogy. Professional development is sometimes called continuing professional development as it is sustained and fluid; educators don't expect children to stop learning and neither should they. There is a great deal of knowledge and expertise that new teachers can learn from more experienced colleagues. However, this shouldn't be the only place they seek development from; as the report states, 'in an effective professional learning system, school leaders learn from experts, mentors, and their peers about how to become true instructional leaders' (Wei et al., 2009: 3). Although this statement mentions school leaders, this kind of approach would suit any teaching professional. I have often maintained that teachers of all levels are leaders in their own classrooms.

Some of the best CPD I have attended has involved external experts visiting the school to train teachers on an aspect of behaviour or cognitive science; however, Fullan (2007: 35) argues that sometimes external approaches are not 'powerful enough, specific enough, or sustained enough to alter the culture of the classroom and school'. The issue is that sometimes schools can try to lift policies from other schools which have completely different contexts or rush through changes without the reflection needed on how they can be implemented. As Elmore (2004: 73) asserts, 'improvement above all entails "learning to do the right things in the setting where you work"'. Some of the best kinds of development might be the opportunities that come from a personal reflection on what the students need and what our own personal development needs are, which is why Easton (2008: 756) refers to the process as professional learning, not professional development: 'educators must be knowledgeable and wise. They must know enough in order to change. They must change in order to get different results. They must become learners, and they must be self-developing.'

Yet, research has shown that professional development is most effective when it is not conducted in isolation; collaborative approaches have been found to be most effective in instigating school change (Newman and Wehlage, 1997). Sometimes working in just one department can be restrictive, so collaborating with other colleagues will provide teachers with a broader sense of understanding, while also serving as a support for improving one another's practice. Moreover, the 'knowledge' element of professional learning has been prominent in recent years due to the increased focus on the importance of teachers' subject knowledge. According to Saxe et al. (2001: 70), there needs to be a 'focused support for teachers' subject matter knowledge and implementation of reform-oriented pedagogical practices'. This is why it is important for your department to also provide opportunities for the expansion of subject knowledge. There are many ways that NQTs can be encouraged to do this themselves, which will be discussed in more detail later on in this chapter.

Engaging with academic research is a further way that teachers can develop professionally, but there is so much of it out there! Navigating what is evidence informed and what may work for a particular context is incredibly difficult, which is why it is essential to engage with it critically and discuss the conclusions with more experienced colleagues. Although wider support networks such as Twitter are fantastic for gaining access to some of this research, it is important to remember that some of the articles that the big education 'celebrities' share may be endorsed because they align with that individual's ideology rather than the research being particularly groundbreaking or robust. This is why engaging with research might be seen by some teachers as being too confusing or contentious. However, grassroots organisations such as researchED and BrewEd have opened up a world of research to teachers in the form of events and videos, making it more practical and applicable than some of the beard stroking discourse that goes on in certain academic circles.

Many of these conferences and events take place at evenings and weekends, and while teachers are not forced to engage with them, thousands of teachers, including me, have chosen to do so. CPD is more fluid than it has been traditionally, so some teachers enjoy doing things in their own time that contribute to their professional development; it is what Wei et al. (2009: 158) refer to as a 'blurring of boundaries between personal and professional development'. An excellent paper by Leat et al. (2013) examines the views and perspectives of those who engage with teacher research. Many practitioners questioned were positive about their experiences, claiming that it provided 'an acceleration of professional understanding and new perspectives which re-invigorate those teachers who do engage' (Leat at al., 2013: 2). Of course, teachers need to be given the time to engage with research and schools need to value it, but this seems to have improved in recent years, with most schools organising their professional development structures around more evidence informed strategies and ideas.

Being a reflective practitioner is an important aspect of being a teacher – knowing our own strengths and areas for development is vital if we want to improve. Teachers, by their nature, seem to be quite reflective – how many of us have found ourselves replaying an event in our head that happened earlier in the day and considering how we could have dealt with it differently? The term 'reflective practice' first emerged in the work of Dewey (1910: 6), who observed that reflective meant possessing a questioning approach. We consider why things are as they are and how they might be different, and also how to 'direct our actions with foresight … It enables us to know what we are about when we act.' For such an old text, the ideas are still relevant to teaching today: what you do in the classroom should be carefully planned, purposeful and informed by theory and experience.

In 1983, Schön expanded these ideas about reflection into two categories: reflection-in-action and reflection-on-action. Reflection-in-action is similar to the adaptive teaching that we explored in Chapter 5, where you might notice something happening (such as students not understanding a topic you are teaching), consider why it is happening and respond to it by changing your approach. In contrast, reflection-on-action is more about when you consider what happened later on, when you are no longer in the classroom. It is more reflective as you have time to think more deeply about the reasons why the students did not understand and why you chose to react in a certain way. Schön also suggests that the way we react depends on our levels of knowledge and experience, so the role of a mentor is significant in helping early career teachers to gain the knowledge they need to become reflective practitioners. Reflective practice is central when it comes to CPD: it can be used as a learning tool which helps us to explain our experiences and identify areas where we need to develop as professionals.

Linked to this idea of self-awareness, a review from the Teacher Development Trust (Cordingley et al., 2015) found that development programmes which provided differentiation, in recognising that teachers start from different points and levels of expertise, are the most successful. The report recommends that schools should support teachers to identify and understand their own needs, and give teachers time to reflect on these, making tacit links to the content of CPD in relation to these needs. Professional development needs to have buy-in potential: the training should be relevant to its participants and their experiences and aspirations. If it does, teachers will engage more deeply in the learning – and if they do, it is more likely to make a difference to the students.

What teachers do in the classroom is usually seen as the most important part of the job; however, professional learning is not just confined to formal development opportunities. There are plenty of opportunities for informal professional development such as getting involved in the broader activities of the school. These may include school trips, running afterschool or lunchtime clubs or helping out at an event. Some of the most joyous experiences I've had as a teacher have been when I've been supporting the school in this way – they truly made me feel part of the school family. Professional learning is not just confined to formal development. These activities also offer a chance to work with other colleagues with whom you may not have worked before and to learn from them.

Robinson (2014) writes about how informal professional development opportunities can bring professional communities of teachers together and how their identities as a teacher can be shaped through this engagement. She interviews teachers who are at many different phases in their careers and almost all of them overwhelmingly reveal that they learn a lot from working with more experienced colleagues: 'Learning from others, particularly heads of departments, deputy heads and head teachers, who could share their professional expertise or just encourage less experienced teachers towards meeting other people, making connections with local authority advisors and promoting certain opportunities, was an important part of their professional development for a number of participants' (Robinson, 2014: 165).

As this quote implies, part of the professional behaviour of teachers includes building effective relationships with parents, carers and families. Research has shown that having a good relationship between home and school can have positive effects on students' achievement, particularly those who struggle with literacy and the academic demands of school (Hughes and Oi-man, 2007). Other studies have also shown that higher levels of home–school conferencing and shared perceptions of children's learning are more likely to lead to congruent positive relationships (Minke et al., 2014). Building these strong relationships can even help teachers to stay at the same school, as those who do so find their job more engaging and fulfilling (Bryk et al., 2010). It is a pity that schools sometimes believe that families and parents need to be managed and held at arm's length, but in a later section of this chapter we will explore how they can be reached out to and engaged with more effectively.

As we have seen, TAs are valuable colleagues and knowing the best ways of working with them is a vital part of a teacher's professional responsibilities. Poor TA deployment has a negative impact on attainment, whereas effective deployment has very positive impacts (EEF, 2018b). There are over 380,000 TAs in England's schools, so it is important that schools get it right! The EEF suggest that students make the most progress when teachers and TAs coordinate to respond to students' real time needs in an immediate and focused way. Their report includes specific strategies on how best to deploy your TA and there are also some practical ideas in the 'How can I help my mentee meet this standard?' section of this chapter.

Engaging and valuing the expertise of other colleagues is also key to ensuring that the appropriate support is there for students. This includes pastoral staff, librarians and careers advisors. Careers education is crucial: if it is effective, it can enable students to explore career options and help them to see how what they are doing in school may open up new opportunities, thereby making the learning more relevant and exciting. The way that teenagers think about their futures has a significant impact on what they go on to do as working adults (EEF, 2016a), so it is essential that teachers work with other professionals to help students visualise what they might become and then inspire and empower them to achieve it.

Focus group findings

Participants in the group spoke about how helpful their mentors had been in suggesting further reading they could do about their professional responsibilities, but many stated that they didn't feel they had received any specific support on how to build effective working relationships. Instead, they felt that this was something they were expected to learn and build on their own. Some new teachers thought that this was something that should be discussed more in their training years.

However, nearly all the early career teachers involved felt they were encouraged to be reflective by exploring issues themselves with a little bit of guidance from their mentors. One teacher said, 'One of my mentors would rarely speak during our regular reflection meetings, rather prompting and teasing out more information from me. It allowed me to become a much more effective practitioner by asking and simultaneously answering my own questions, instead of always being given information and being told what to do. It was a much more effective way to be mentored and has allowed me to grow into an efficient reflective teacher. They gave me the support and demonstrated many of the skills and attributes I would ideally need to adopt, without forcing or insisting that I mirrored anything they did. They modelled good practice and subtly encouraged me to take on such behaviours.'

Some felt that their mentors were too 'uptight' about the particulars of what their NQTs were doing, particularly small things such as what colour paper they used or how often they gave written feedback in books. However, the better mentors they had experienced were more realistic: although they insisted on department non-negotiables, they also realised that teachers aren't perfect and they sometimes get things wrong.

The best mentors were those who made the NQTs feel like professional teachers by encouraging them to have a voice, get involved and be trusted to do their job. One teacher said, 'My mentor encouraged me to get involved in departmental discussions. Since my subject knowledge was strong, I always felt I had something to add, but without his encouragement bringing me into those discussions I would not have had the courage to dive in on my own. It made a huge difference to my own confidence in finding my voice as a colleague in the company of other teachers, rather than just in front of the children.'

Most of the participants questioned felt that they had been supported with managing their workload and wellbeing. Although some of them didn't feel as if they'd had any real crises with workload during their first year, they appreciated the help their mentor offered. For example, 'On a week with a parents' evening he would help me make sure I had planned well enough ahead so that I didn't need to stay late any other night. When we had deadlines for estimating grades for GCSE classes, which is difficult as an NQT, we planned out time to go through this together so that I wouldn't be worrying about it outside of school or taking too long trying to get it done on my own.'

Some teachers spoke about how other teachers in their school or department hadn't been as helpful, and how well-meaning comments about workload could sometimes make them feel more anxious. One participant said, 'I found that there are lots of people who will call out "Don't stay too late!" as they walk out past you in the middle of lots of jobs, but that isn't a very helpful comment. Those who spout, "I never work in the evening or at the weekend", aren't helpful either; it just makes the new teacher feel inefficient and inadequate for working late. The helpful people are those who say, "I saw you were here late last night – what were you doing? How can we help you to organise your time so that you leave on time today?" or "If anybody is going to struggle getting all of their classes marked by day X, then please just drop me an email – I want you all to have a weekend." It's not about being a martyr and working all the hours God sends, but it's also not about pretending that it's easy to get everything done well and leave at 4pm each day.'

How can I help my mentee meet this standard?

Part of helping your NQT to develop as a professional is teaching them how to be reflective. Some people are naturally predisposed to do this, whereas others may find it more difficult. When I first came into teaching I definitely belonged to the latter group. I had joined the profession from the pontificating, blustering, arrogant world of national newspaper journalism, where people didn't reflect on their own weaknesses or behaviours, they just sought to cover them up and shout about their successes. It wasn't long before I was taken down a peg or two, and while I wouldn't promote this as a strategy for mentors, it did me the world of good. However, a mentor can help their mentee to become more reflective by guiding and encouraging them to embrace feedback and criticism and to reflect on their teaching.

In an earlier chapter, I advocated asking your NQT to observe you and provide feedback on an aspect of your teaching. This is also important here and a useful exercise to model the kind of reflective behaviours you expect to see from a new teacher when they receive feedback. It is also worth looking at some models of reflection and using them as scaffolds to support reflection-on-action. There are many different options, such as Boud's triangular representation or the Atkins and Murphy model, but personally I prefer Gibb's reflective cycle (Figure 8.1) as it is made up of a series of questions that the teacher can reflect on which are specific but can be interpreted in many different ways.

Figure 8.1. Gibb's reflective cycle (adapted from Dye, 2011)

Using these questions instead of the vague 'How do you think the lesson went?' after an observation can help to promote deeper reflection, as the NQT can start to formulate alternatives and ways forward. To promote this open and trusting relationship, your mentee needs to respect you and know that you are committed to helping them improve – and part of this is about looking at the positives and focusing on their strengths. This relationship is also helped if there is a willingness to learn from both of you; although you are the expert colleague, you can still learn together. Even though NQTs are not subject to school performance management procedures, if the standards are used properly they should identify areas of weakness in a new teacher's practice, which means that you can both focus on developing that specific standard with clear intentions of how they can practise this skill to impact positively on student outcomes. An example of this might be that they are not contributing to the wider life of the school, so you could help them to find opportunities to do this by introducing them to other colleagues, such as the teacher who runs the Duke of Edinburgh's Award or the teacher who runs the school production. Initially, they may not feel confident enough to seek these colleagues out themselves or even know where to start.

Part of this learning together may take place when attending school CPD sessions or strengthening pedagogical and subject knowledge by participating in wider networks. There are so many opportunities to do this now, from engaging with Twitter to joining a subject association, watching webinars or attending conferences. My own school has bought new teachers a ticket to both the researchED national conference and Blackpool events every year and their mentors have attended with them. Although there has been some recent negativity about researchED, in my opinion it is still one of the events that has developed me most as a teacher due to the sheer volume of expertise from fellow practitioners and their willingness to share with others. There are also many other smaller, grassroots style conferences which are a bit more informal, such as local BrewEd events which are held in pubs and combine pints and pedagogy.[1]

The Education Endowment Foundation is also a useful starting point as they helpfully summarise research and key topics and produce guidance reports with clear recommendations that teachers can easily implement. Their network of research schools is another resource to tap into as they run professional development opportunities, although they can be a bit insular. The Chartered College of Teaching is an interesting organisation for your NQT to join: they publish very useful articles and resources both on their website and in their magazine, *Impact*.[2] They strike a great balance between academic content and practical application and also give teachers a sense of identity and collegiate support by being part of the professional body for educators. Reading articles in *Impact* or other educational journals will encourage your mentee to engage with the research. If you then discuss the ideas you both read together, this will help them to see how the research is relevant to their practice and will help them to improve.

But engaging with research is about more than just swallowing recommendations and findings whole; this is why navigating academic research can be so tricky. It is important to examine it with a critical eye to see whether it is robust. Onwuegbuzie and Frels (2016) set out some criteria for teachers to consider when assessing the usefulness of an information source:

- Authenticity: how trustworthy is the source?
- Merit: how knowledgeable, respected and competent is the author?

---

1   You can find out about the next events on their websites: https://researched.org.uk and https://just-brewed.org.
2   See https://chartered.college.

- Validity of the evidence: is it rooted in quantitative research?
- Credibility of the evidence: if it is qualitative research, how believable are the findings?
- Rigorous research practices: does it adhere to academic standards?
- External validity: can the results be generalised?

Although these kinds of considerations and conversations are more often undertaken in universities or during training years, as the number of teachers utilising and engaging with research increases, they are also important to consider when mentoring young teachers who may have their practice shaped by false information which peddles itself as academic research, such as learning styles. It is useful to keep these questions in mind whenever you are discussing research.

Different schools and departments may have policies and procedures when communicating with parents. Obviously, these must be adhered to, but there are ways that an NQT can engage with parents. Making that first contact can be stressful, but most parents are supportive and open to communications from school. Don't get me wrong: I have had encounters with parents that have been extremely challenging – bordering on abusive – but we have worked hard to reconcile our differences, as ultimately we both have the best interests of the child at heart and are working towards a common good. The organisation School Home Support (2015) have published useful guidance about what schools should be doing to communicate successfully with parents and carers. They recommend that:

- Communication between school and home should be regular, meaningful and two way.
- Parents must be given the tools and means to effectively support their children's educational needs so they can be actively involved in the process.
- Parents should be partners in decisions made about their children and this collaboration will enhance student learning.

Many parents have become home educators during the COVID-19 pandemic, so they have more of an insight into what subjects and topics their children are studying in school. However, some parents, like me, may have realised that they are inadequately equipped to help their children in certain subjects as they do not possess the necessary skills or knowledge. The head of maths at my current school recognised that maths is sometimes a barrier for parents. He organised a workshop where he taught parents some of the key GCSE concepts, so they then felt empowered to assist their children with their work at home. This was a massive success. If you wanted to involve your NQT in a project to develop their working relationships with parents, you could organise something like this or together create some resources and materials for parents. There are many useful ideas in the School Home Support toolkit that you could explore together.

Schools are made up of many different colleagues who all play important roles in developing students, so it is essential that new teachers know who these colleagues are and how they can work with them to meet the needs of the learners. Some schools have a virtual learning environment including a 'who's who' of staff, complete with photos, job titles and telephone extensions. Other schools don't, so if your school falls into this category, it may be beneficial to provide your NQT with this information so they know who is the SENDCO, exams officer, careers advisor, safeguarding lead and so on. They need to know that all staff are part of a team and that, if needed, they are entitled to ask for help and support from anyone in the team. This includes knowing the procedures for reporting safeguarding concerns and how to record them.

Best practice in deploying TAs was discussed in Chapter 5, but as the working relationship between teacher and TA is so important, it will be explored further here. In their guidance report, the EEF (2018b) give seven key recommendations to guide teachers in how to utilise the precious resource of the TA (Table 8.1). Some of these focus on things that teachers and TAs can do prior to and during lessons, but the last one focuses on how teachers can build explicit links between interventions that students may be having outside of lessons and what they are doing in class. This is why communication is key: if a teacher is not aware of interventions, they would find this impossible to do. Meeting with the SENDCO or the TA who regularly works with that student will reveal useful information which will help the new teacher plan to meet their needs. It is beneficial if you can assist with organising these meetings and ensure that the NQT is given time to do this.

Table 8.1. TA deployment recommendations (adapted from EEF, 2018b: 3)

TAs in the classroom	
1	TAs should not only be used as a resource for lower attaining pupils.
2	TAs should add value to what the teacher does, not replace them.
3	TAs should help students to become more independent and be able to manage their own learning.

| 4 | TAs need to be fully briefed and prepared for their role in the classroom. |

Structured interventions out of class

| 5 | TAs should be used to give high quality, small group and individual support using structured interventions. |
| 6 | Interventions should be evidence based. |

Integrating classroom and intervention learning

| 7 | Connections between interventions and classroom learning should be explicitly linked. |

Finally, supporting your NQT with their wellbeing and managing their workload is arguably one of a mentor's most important jobs. At the beginning of this book, I set out what the NQTs I interviewed said about what they felt makes a good mentor; invariably there was a response which involved some kind of empathetic or caring quality. At times you will be a shoulder to cry on or an understanding ear. You may be someone they can vent their frustrations to or share successes with. Perhaps, most importantly, you will be instrumental in supporting them to stay in the profession, and one aspect of that is helping them to become more efficient with their time and task management skills. It is about teaching them to work smarter, not harder. Encouraging new teachers to use different forms of feedback and to keep on top of tasks during PPA will help, as well as persuading them not to reinvent the wheel and to collaborate with colleagues to share planning or use resources from textbooks rather than spending valuable time on this. It is key that mentors lead by example, so try not to stay in school working late into the night yourself or the new teacher will see this as the norm. It is essential to show new teachers that they do not need to be martyrs and that they should look after number one, because a tired teacher will not be at the top of their game.

Teaching is such an all-encompassing job that it is often referred to as a vocation rather than a profession. I find this to be an unhelpful narrative: I am convinced that the pressure put on teachers to work 60-plus hours a week is a factor in the poor retention rates. Instead, it is our job as mentors to encourage new teachers to strike a manageable work–life balance, and also to give themselves time to rest and recover rather than sending themselves under by working constantly. Help them to prioritise their workload by making lists, deciding what is crucial for them to complete and looking at ways they can save time by using pre-existing resources and routines.

NQTs are the lifeblood of a school with their dynamic and vibrant ideas, but they are also some of the most vulnerable. We need to understand that they are not the finished product and that our strategic support will shape them into the teachers they will become. We owe it to them and future generations of students to offer them the support, guidance and professional development opportunities they need in order to feel enthused, valued and motivated to stay in the profession for many years to come.

Chapter 8: Summary

Identify goal:
To understand that effective professional development is sustained over time and includes input from experts and opportunities for collaboration. Teachers need to be reflective and to act on feedback. They also need to build effective working relationships with parents and wider colleagues to ensure that students are adequately supported.

Evaluate and reflect on the standard:
- Does the NQT now have an understanding about how to fulfil their wider professional responsibilities?
- Ask them to rate their confidence and identify areas where they need more support.
- Create an action plan for further reading and next steps to develop their skills.

Standard 8
– Fulfil wider professional responsibilities

Apply the learning:
- Use Gibb's reflective cycle (Figure 8.1) to reflect on some of the NQT's lessons.
- Read School Home Support's (2015) suggestions for engaging with parents and encourage the new teacher to trial some of the strategies.
- Help the early career teacher to manage their workload by sharing hints and tips to maximise output.
- Be there to listen to your NQT and always be open, honest and positive and have a solutions focused approach.

Come up with a plan:

- Discuss with your mentee what it means to be reflective and encourage them to see the value of feedback and constructive criticism.
- Consider whether there may be opportunities for the new teacher to get involved in wider school life, such as trips or events, and make the necessary introductions.
- Together explore the websites of researchED, BrewEd, the EEF's research schools and the Chartered College of Teaching to see what events and resources are on offer.
- Create a who's who of key staff, complete with pictures and telephone extensions, so your NQT can easily ask for help and support when needed.

Learn together:

- Encourage the new teacher to observe your teaching and give you some feedback, so you can model how teachers can be reflective.
- Attend some conferences or CPD events together.
- Read a copy of *Impact* independently and discuss how some of the findings could be integrated into both of your practice.
- Explore some journal articles and use Onwuegbuzie and Frels' (2016) principles to discuss whether the evidence and findings in them are robust.

Bibliography

Alexander, R. J. (2003) *Talk for Learning: The First Year*. Available at: http://robinalexander. org.uk/wp-content/uploads/2019/12/North-Yorks-report-03.pdf.

Alexander, R. J. (2005) *Teaching Through Dialogue: The First Year*. London: Barking and Dagenham Council.

Alexander, R. J. (2008) *Towards Dialogic Teaching: Rethinking Classroom Talk*. Thirsk: Dialogos UK.

Alexander, R. J. (2020) *A Dialogic Teaching Companion*. Abingdon and New York: Routledge.

Allen, M. J. (2004) *Assessing Academic Programs in Higher Education*. San Francisco, CA: Jossey-Bass.

Assessment Reform Group (1999) *Assessment for Learning: Beyond the Black Box*. Available at: https://www.nuffieldfoundation.org/sites/default/files/files/beyond_blackbox.pdf.

Atkinson, R. K., Derry, S. J., Renkl, A. and Wortham, D. (2000) 'Learning from examples: instructional principles from the worked examples research'. *Review of Educational Research*, 70: 181–214.

Bahrick, H. P. and Hall, L. K. (2005) 'The importance of retrieval failures to long-term retention: a metacognitive explanation of the spacing effect'. *Journey of Memory and Language*, 52: 566–577.

Barrett, P. S., Zhang, Y., Davies, F. and Barrett, L. C. (2015) *Clever Classrooms: Summary Report of The HEAD Project*. Salford: University of Salford. Available at: http://usir.salford.ac. uk/id/eprint/35221/1/120515%20Clever%20Classrooms.pdf.

Bartlett, F. C. (1932) *Remembering: A Study in Experimental and Social Psychology*. Oxford: Macmillan.

Battistich, V., Schaps, E., Watson, M., Solomon, D. and Lewis, C. (2000) 'Effects of the Child Development Project on students' drug use and other problem behaviors'. *Journal of Primary Prevention*, 2(1): 75–79.

Battistich, V., Schaps, E. and Wilson, N. (2004) 'Effects of an elementary school intervention on students' "connectedness" to school and social adjustment during middle school'. *Journal of Primary Prevention*, 24(3): 243–262.

Bennett, T. (2017) *Creating a Culture: How School Leaders Can Optimise Behaviour*. Available at: https://assets.publishing.service.gov.uk/government/uploads/system/uploads/ attachment_data/file/602487/Tom_Bennett_Independent_Review_of_Behaviour_in_ Schools.pdf.

Biggs, J. (1987) *Student Approaches to Learning and Studying*. Melbourne: Australian Council for Educational Research.

Bircher, R. (2013) 'Are textbooks out of fashion?' *Oxford Education Blog* (9 December). Available at: https://educationblog.oup.com/secondary/psychology/are-textbooks-out-of-fashion.

Black P. and Wiliam, D. (1998) *Inside the Black Box: Raising Standards Through Classroom Assessment.* London: King's College London.

Black, P. and Wiliam, D. (2001) 'Inside the black box: raising standards through classroom assessment'. Available at: https://weaeducation.typepad.co.uk/files/blackbox-1.pdf.

Bor, D. (2012) *The Ravenous Brain: How the New Science of Consciousness Explains Our Insatiable Search for Meaning.* New York: Basic Books.

Bourdieu, P. and Passeron, J. C. (1977) *Reproduction in Education, Society and Culture.* London: SAGE.

Bradbury, A. (2011) 'Rethinking assessment and inequality: the production of disparities in attainment in early years education'. *Journal of Education Policy*, 26(5): 655–676.

Bryk, A., Sebring, P., Allensworth, E., Luppescu, S. and Easton, J. (2010) *Organizing Schools for Improvement.* Chicago, IL: University of Chicago Press.

Bullough, R. and Baughman, K. (1997) *An Inquiry into Teacher Development.* New York: Teachers College Press.

Campbell, T. (2015) 'Stereotyped at seven? Biases in teacher judgement of pupils' ability and attainment'. *Journal of Social Policy*, 44(3): 517–547.

Carpenter, S. K. (2009) 'Cue strength as a moderator of the testing effect: the benefits of elaborative retrieval'. *Journal of Experimental Psychology: Learning, Memory and Cognition*, 35: 1563–1569.

Carpenter, S. K., Pashler, H. and Cepeda, N. J. (2008) 'Using tests to enhance 8th grade students' retention of U.S. history facts'. *Applied Cognitive Psychology*, 23(6): 760–771.

Carroll, J., Bradley, L., Crawford, H., Hannant, P., Johnson, H. and Thompson, A. (2017) *SEN Support: A Rapid Evidence Assessment.* Available at: https://assets.publishing.service.gov.uk/government/uploads/system/uploads/attachment_data/file/628630/DfE_SEN_Support_REA_Report.pdf.

Caviglioli, O. (2015) 'PowerPoint presentations'. *How To* (30 November). Available at: https://teachinghow2s.com/blog/powerpoint-presentations.

Caviglioli, O. (2019a) *Dual Coding with Teachers.* Woodbridge: John Catt Educational.

Caviglioli, O. (2019b) 'The Principles of Instruction' [poster]. Available at: https://cdn.teachinghow2s.com/docs/Principles_of_Instruction_Barak_Rosenshine.pdf.

Cepeda, N. J., Coburn, N., Rohrer, D., Wixted, J. T., Mozer, M. C. and Pashler, H. (2009) 'Optimizing distributed practice: theoretical analysis and practical implications'. *Experimental Psychology*, 56(4): 236–246.

Chapman, R. L., Buckley, L., Sheehan, M. C., Shochet, I. M. and Romaniuk, M. (2011) 'The impact of school connectedness on violent behavior, transport risk-taking behavior, and associated injuries in adolescence'. *Journal of School Psychology*, 49(4): 399–410.

Chi, M. T. H, de Leeuw, N., Chiu, M. H. and LaVancher, C. (1994) 'Eliciting self-explanations improves understanding'. *Cognitive Science*, 18: 439–477.

Christodoulou, D. (2017) 'How can we measure progress in lessons?' (11 February). Available at: https://daisychristodoulou.com/2017/02/how-can-we-measure-progress-in-lessons.

Christodoulou, D. (2018) 'Comparative judgement: the next big revelation in assessment'. *researchED* (6 July). Available at: https://researched.org.uk/comparative-judgement-the-next-big-revolution-in-assessment.

Coe, R., Aloisi, C., Higgins, S. and Major, L. E. (2014) *What Makes Great Teaching? Review of the Underpinning Research.* Available at: https://www.suttontrust.com/wp-content/uploads/2014/10/What-Makes-Great-Teaching-REPORT.pdf.

Cohen, E. G. (1994) 'Restructuring the classroom: conditions for productive small groups'. *Review of Educational Research,* 64: 1–35.

Cordingley, P., Higgins, S., Greany, T., Buckler, N., Coles-Jordan, D., Crisp, B., Saunders, L. and Coe, R. (2015) *Developing Great Teaching: Lessons from the International Reviews Into Effective Professional Development.* Available at: https://tdtrust.org/about/dgt.

Counsell, C. (2018) 'Senior curriculum leadership 1: the indirect manifestation of knowledge: (A) curriculum as narrative'. *The Dignity of the Thing* (7 April). Available at: https://thedignityofthethingblog.wordpress.com/2018/04/07/senior-curriculum-leadership-1-the-indirect-manifestation-of-knowledge-a-curriculum-as-narrative.

Cull, W. L. (2000) 'Untangling the opportunities of multiple study opportunities and repeated testing for cued recall'. *Applied Cognitive Psychology,* 14: 215–235.

Danielson, C. (2007) *Enhancing Professional Practice: A Framework for Teaching.* Alexandria, VA: Association for Supervision and Curriculum Development.

Davis, P., Florian, L., Ainscow, M., Dyson, A., Farrell, P., Hick, P. and Rouse, M. (2004) *Teaching Strategies and Approaches for Pupils with Special Educational Needs: A Scoping Study.* Nottingham: Department for Education and Skills. Available at: https://dera.ioe.ac.uk/6059/1/RR516.pdf.

Department for Education (2011) *Teachers' Standards: Guidance for School Leaders, School Staff and Governing Bodies* (July). Ref: DFE-00066-2011. Available at: https://www.gov.uk/government/publications/teachers-standards.

Department for Education (2014a) *The National Curriculum in England: Framework Document* (December). Available at: https://assets.publishing.service.gov.uk/government/uploads/system/uploads/attachment_data/file/381344/Master_final_national_curriculum_28_Nov.pdf.

Department for Education (2014b) *SEND Code of Practice* (January). Available at: https://assets.publishing.service.gov.uk/government/uploads/system/uploads/attachment_data/file/398815/SEND_Code_of_Practice_January_2015.pdf.

Department for Education (2019) *Early Career Framework* (January). Available at: https://www.gov.uk/government/publications/early-career-framework.

Department for Education (2020) *Initial Teacher Training (ITT): Core Content Framework* (November). Available at: https://www.gov.uk/government/publications/initial-teacher-training-itt-core-content-framework.

Dewey, J. (1910) *How We Think.* London: D.C. Heath.

Didau, D. (2011) 'Some thoughts on learning styles'. *The Learning Spy* (5 December). Available at: https://learningspy.co.uk/learning/some-thoughts-on-learning-styles-2.

Didau, D. (2015) 'Is displaying students' work worth the effort?' *The Learning Spy* (16 May). Available at: https://learningspy.co.uk/myths/is-displaying-students-work-worth-the-effort-2.

Didau, D. (2016) 'One more nail in the learning styles coffin'. *The Learning Spy* (19 February). Available at: https://learningspy.co.uk/myths/whats-the-difference-between-modalities-and-learning-styles.

Dix, P. (2017) *When the Adults Change, Everything Changes: Seismic Shifts in School Behaviour.* Carmarthen: Independent Thinking Press.

Dunlosky, J., Rawson, K. A., Marsh, E. J., Nathan, M. J. and Willingham, D. T. (2013) 'Improving students' learning with effective learning techniques: promising directions from cognitive and educational psychology'. *Psychological Science in the Public Interest*, 14(1): 4–58.

DuPaul, G. J. and Weyandt, L. L. (2006) 'School-based interventions for children and adolescents with attention deficit/hyperactivity disorder: enhancing academic and behavioral outcomes'. *Education and Treatment of Children*, 29(2): 341–358.

Dweck, C. S. (2008) 'Brainology: transforming students' motivation to learn'. *National Association of Independent Schools*. Available at: https://www.nais.org/magazine/independent-school/winter-2008/brainology.

Dye, V. (2011) 'Reflection, reflection, reflection. I'm thinking all the time, why do I need a theory or model of reflection?' In D. McGregor and L. Cartwright (eds), *Developing Reflective Practice: A Guide for Beginning Teachers*. Maidenhead: McGraw-Hill Education, pp. 217–234.

Earp, B. D. (2010) 'Automatically in the classroom: unconscious mental processes and the racial achievement gap'. *Journal of Multiculturalism in Education*, 6(1): 1–22.

Easton, L. B. (2008) 'From professional development to professional learning'. *Phi Delta Kappan*, 89(10): 755–759.

Education Endowment Foundation (EEF) (2016a) *Careers Education: International Literature Review*. Available at: https://educationendowmentfoundation.org.uk/public/files/Presentations/Publications/Careers_review.pdf.

Education Endowment Foundation (EEF) (2016b) *Improving Literacy in Key Stage 1: Guidance Report*. Available at: https://educationendowmentfoundation.org.uk/tools/guidance-reports/literacy-ks-1.

Education Endowment Foundation (EEF) (2017) *Improving Literacy in Key Stage 2: Guidance Report*. Available at: https://educationendowmentfoundation.org.uk/tools/guidance-reports/literacy-ks-2.

Education Endowment Foundation (EEF) (2018a) *Embedding Formative Assessment: Evaluation Report and Executive Summary*. Available at: https://educationendowmentfoundation.org.uk/public/files/EFA_evaluation_report.pdf.

Education Endowment Foundation (EEF) (2018b) *Making Best Use of Teaching Assistants: Guidance Report*. Available at: https://educationendowmentfoundation.org.uk/public/files/Publications/Teaching_Assistants/TA_Guidance_Report_MakingBestUseOfTeachingAssistants-Printable.pdf.

Education Endowment Foundation (EEF) (2018c) *Metacognition and Self-Regulated Learning: Guidance Report*. Available at: https://educationendowmentfoundation.org.uk/public/files/Publications/Metacognition/EEF_Metacognition_and_self-regulated_learning.pdf.

Education Endowment Foundation (EEF) (2018d) '15 key lessons learned in the EEF's first six years' (23 January). Available at: https://educationendowmentfoundation.org.uk/news/15-key-lessons-learned-in-the-eefs-first-six-years.

Education Endowment Foundation (EEF) (2018e) 'Mastery learning evidence summary' (23 August). Available at: https://educationendowmentfoundation.org.uk/evidence-summaries/teaching-learning-toolkit/mastery-learning.

Education Endowment Foundation (EEF) (2018f) 'Learning styles: Teaching and Learning Toolkit' (29 August). Available at: https://educationendowmentfoundation.org.uk/ evidence-summaries/teaching-learning-toolkit/learning-styles.

Education Endowment Foundation (EEF) (2018g) 'Collaborative learning: Teaching and Learning Toolkit' (13 November). Available at: https://educationendowmentfoundation.org. uk/evidence-summaries/teaching-learning-toolkit/collaborative-learning.

Education Endowment Foundation (EEF) (2019) *Improving Literacy in Secondary Schools: Guidance Report*. Available at: https://educationendowmentfoundation.org.uk/public/files/ Publications/Literacy/EEF_KS3_KS4_LITERACY_GUIDANCE.pdf.

Education Endowment Foundation (EEF) (2020) 'Homework (secondary): Teaching and Learning Toolkit' (16 April). Available at: https://educationendowmentfoundation.org.uk/ evidence-summaries/teaching-learning-toolkit/homework-secondary.

Education Support Partnership (2018) *Teacher Wellbeing Index 2018*. Available at: https:// www.educationsupport.org.uk/sites/default/files/teacher_wellbeing_index_2018.pdf.

Elliott, V., Baird, J-A., Hopfenbeck, T. N., Ingram, J., Thompson, I., Usher, N. and Zantouto, M. (2016) *A Marked Improvement? A Review of the Evidence on Written Marking*. Available at: https://educationendowmentfoundation.org.uk/public/files/Presentations/Publications/ EEF_Marking_Review_April_2016.pdf.

Elmore, R. F. (2004) *School Reform from the Inside Out*. Cambridge, MA: Harvard University Press.

Enser, M. (2017) 'How can we create a culture of excellence in schools?' *The Guardian* (2 August). Available at: https://www.theguardian.com/teacher-network/teacher-blog/2017/ aug/02/create-culture-excellence-schools-students-teachers.

Epstein, M., Atkins, M., Cullinan, D., Kutash, K. and Weaver, R. (2008) *Reducing Behavior Problems in the Elementary School Classroom: A Practice Guide*. NCEE #2008-012. Washington, DC: National Center for Education Evaluation and Regional Assistance, Institute of Education Sciences and US Department of Education. Available at: https://ies.ed.gov/ ncee/wwc/PracticeGuide/4.

Fisher, A., Godwin, K. E. and Seltman, H. (2014) 'Visual environment, attention allocation, and learning in young children: when too much of a good thing may be bad'. *Psychology Science*, 25(7): 1362–1370.

Fisher, D. and Frey, N. (2010) 'Identifying instructional moves during guided learning'. *The Reading Teacher*, 64(2): 84–95.

Ford, M. (1992) *Motivating Humans: Goals, Emotions, and Personal Agency Beliefs*. London: SAGE.

Fullan, M. (2007) 'Change the terms for teacher learning'. *Journal of Staff Development*, 28(3): 35–36.

Gathercole, S. E. and Alloway, T. P. (2008) *Working Memory and Learning: A Practical Guide*. London: SAGE.

Gathercole, S. E. and Pickering, S. J. (2000) 'Assessment of working memory in six- and seven-year-old children'. *Journal of Educational Psychology*, 92: 377–390.

Gibson, S., Oliver, L. and Dennison, M. (2015) *Workload Challenge: Analysis of Teacher Consultation Responses*. Research report (February). Available at: https://www.gov.uk/ government/publications/workload-challenge-analysis-of-teacher-responses.

Goodenow, C. (1993) 'The psychological sense of school membership among adolescents: scale development and educational correlates'. *Psychology in the Schools*, 30: 79–90.

Gregory, A., Hafen, C. A., Ruzek, E., Mikami, A. Y., Allen, J. P. and Pianta, R. C. (2016) 'Closing the racial discipline gap in classrooms by changing teacher practice'. *School Psychological Review*, 45(2): 171–191.

Grotberg, E. (1995) 'A guide to promoting resilience in children: strengthening the human spirit'. *Early Childhood Development: Practice and Reflections*, 8: 1–43.

Hadwin, A. F., Webster, E., Helm, S., McCardle, L. and Gendron, A. (2010) 'Toward the study of intra-individual differences in goal setting and motivation regulation'. Paper presented at the annual meeting of the American Educational Research Association, Denver, CO, April.

Hamilton, L. (2006) 'Implicit theories of ability: teacher constructs and classroom consequences'. *Scottish Educational Review*, 38(2): 201–212.

Hammond, G. (2018) 'Cognitive load theory in the English classroom'. *The Deep Bare Garden* (29 November). Available at: https://thedeepbaregarden.wordpress.com/2018/11/29/cognitive-load-theory-in-the-english-classroom.

Hamre, B. K. and Pianta, R. C. (2005) 'Can instructional and emotional support in the first-grade classroom make a difference for children at risk of school failure?' *Child Development*, 76: 949–967.

Harris, I. and Caviglioli, O. (2003) *Think It – Map It*. London: A&C Black.

Hattie, J. (1999) 'Influences on student learning'. Inaugural lecture, University of Auckland, 2 August. Available at: https://cdn.auckland.ac.nz/assets/education/about/research/documents/influences-on-student-learning.pdf.

Hattie, J. (2009) *Visible Learning: A Synthesis of Over 800 Meta-Analyses Relating to Achievement*. Abingdon: Routledge.

Hattie, J. (2012) *Visible Learning for Teachers: Maximizing Impact on Learners*. Abingdon and New York: Routledge.

Hattie, J. and Yates, G. C. R. (2014) *Visible Learning and the Science of How We Learn*. Abingdon and New York: Routledge.

Hendrick, C. (2015) 'The scourge of motivational posters and the problem with pop psychology in the classroom'. *Chronotope* (15 February). Available at: https://chronotopeblog.com/2015/02/15/the-scourge-of-motivational-posters-and-the-problem-with-pop-psychology-in-the-classroom.

Hill, H. C., Rowan, B. and Ball, D. L. (2005) 'Effects of teachers' mathematical knowledge for teaching on student achievement'. *American Educational Research Journal*, 42(2): 371–406.

Hoge, R. D. and Cudmore, L. (1986) 'The use of teacher-judgement measures in the identification of gifted pupils'. *Journal of Educational Psychology*, 76: 213–228.

Holloway, J. H. (2001) 'The benefits of mentoring'. *Educational Leadership*, 58(8): 85–86.

Howard-Jones, P., Ioannou, K., Bailey, R., Prior, J., Yau, S. H. and Jay, T. (2018) 'Applying the science of learning in the classroom'. *Impact* (February). Available at: https://impact.chartered.college/article/howard-jones-applying-science-learning-classroom.

Hughes, H. (2020) *Preserving Positivity: Choosing to Stay in the Classroom and Banishing a Negative Mindset*. Woodbridge: John Catt Educational.

Hughes, J. and Oi-man, K. (2007) 'Influence of student–teacher and parent–teacher relationships on lower achieving readers' engagement and achievement in the primary grades'. *Journal of Educational Psychology*, 99(1): 39–51.

Humphrey, N. and Brooks, A. G. (2006) 'An evaluation of a short cognitive-behavioural anger management intervention for pupils at risk of exclusion'. *Emotional and Behavioural Difficulties*, 11(1): 5–23.

Jarvis, H. L. and Gathercole, S. E. (2003) 'Verbal and non-verbal working memory and achievements on national curriculum tests at 11 and 14 years of age'. *Educational and Child Psychology*, 20: 123–140.

Jay, T., Willis, B., Thomas, P., Taylor, R., Moore, N., Burnett, C., Merchant, G. and Stevens, A. (2017) *Dialogic Teaching: Evaluation Report and Executive Summary*. Project Report. London: Education Endowment Foundation.

Kane, M. J., Brown, L. H., McVay, J. C., Silvia, P. J., Myin-Germeys, I. and Kwapil, T. R. (2007) 'For whom the mind wanders, and when: an experience-sampling study of working memory and executive control in daily life'. *Psychological Science*, 18: 614–621.

Kern, L. and Clemens, N. H. (2007) 'Antecedent strategies to promote appropriate classroom behaviour'. *Psychology in the Schools*, 44(1): 65–75.

Kern, L., Gallagher, P., Starosta, K., Hickman, W. and George, M. L. (2006) 'Longitudinal outcomes of functional behavioral assessment-based intervention'. *Journal of Positive Behavior Interventions*, 8: 67–78.

Kerry, T. and Mayes, A. S. (1995) *Issues in Mentoring*. London: Psychology Press.

Kidd, D. (2020) *A Curriculum of Hope: As Rich in Humanity as in Knowledge*. Carmarthen: Independent Thinking Press.

Kirschner, P. A., Sweller, J., Kirschner, F. and Zambrano, J. (2018) 'From cognitive load theory to collaborative cognitive load theory'. *International Journal of Computer Supported Collaborative Learning*, 13: 213–233.

Knight, J. (2016) 'Teach to win: seven success factors for instructional coaching programs'. *Education Digest*, 81(5): 27–32.

Knight, P. (2001) 'Assessment series no. 7: a briefing on key concepts formative and summative, criterion and norm-referenced assessment'. Available at: https://view.officeapps. live.com/op/view.aspx?src=https%3A%2F%2Fblogs.shu.ac. uk%2Fteaching%2Ffiles%2F2016%2F09%2FNo7_briefing_on_key_concepts.docx.

Kraft, M. A., Blazar, D. and Hogan, D. (2018) 'The effect of teacher coaching on instruction and achievement: a meta-analysis of the causal evidence'. *Review of Educational Research*, 88(4): 547–588.

Larsen, S. (2019) 'Visualisers: how they can be used to live model, and give immediate verbal feedback' (24 September). Available at: https://sarahlarsen.school.blog/2019/09/24/ visualisers-how-they-can-be-used-to-live-model-and-give-immediate-verbal-feedback.

Leat, D., Lofthouse, R. and Reid, A. (2013) 'Teachers' views: perspectives on research engagement. Research and teacher education: the BERA-ISA inquiry'. Available at: https:// www.bera.ac.uk/wp-content/uploads/2013/12/BERA-Paper-7-Teachers-Views-Perspectives-on-research-engagement.pdf.

Lee, I. (2019) 'Teacher written corrective feedback: less is more'. *Language Teaching*, 52(4): 524–536.

Lemov, D. (2015) *Teach Like a Champion 2.0: 62 Techniques That Put Students on the Path to College.* San Francisco, CA: Jossey-Bass.

Libbey, H. (2004) 'Measuring student relationships to school: attachment, bonding, connectedness, and engagement'. *Journal of School Health*, 74(7): 274–283.

Loewenberg Ball, D. and Feiman-Nemser, S. (1988) 'Using textbooks and teachers' guides: a dilemma for beginning teachers and teacher educators'. *Curriculum Inquiry*, 18(4): 401–423.

Lyle, S. (2008) 'Learners' collaborative talk'. In M. Martin-Jones, A-M. de Mejia and N. Hornberger (eds), *Encyclopaedia of Language and Education.* Vol. III: *Discourse and Education.* New York: Springer, pp. 279–290.

MacBeath, J. and Turner, M. (1990) 'Learning out of school: homework, policy and practice. A research study commissioned by the Scottish Education Department'. Available at: https://files.eric.ed.gov/fulltext/ED361089.pdf.

McClelland, M., Cameron, C., Wanless, S. and Murray, A. (2007) 'Executive function, behavioral self-regulation, and social-emotional competence: links to school readiness'. In O. N. Saracho and B. Spodek (eds), *Contemporary Perspectives on Research in Social Learning in Early Childhood Education.* Charlotte, NC: Information Age Publishing, pp. 83–107.

McGill, R. M. (2017) *Mark. Plan. Teach: Save Time. Reduce Workload. Impact Learning.* London: Bloomsbury.

McGill, R. M. (2018) '25 years researching teaching and learning'. *@TeacherToolkit* (5 November). Available at: https://www.teachertoolkit.co.uk/2018/11/05/mark-plan-teach-teaching-and-learning.

McInerney, L. (2018) 'What if it's behaviour, not workload, that makes teachers leave?' *Schools Week* (24 September). Available at: https://schoolsweek.co.uk/what-if-its-behaviour-not-workload-that-makes-teachers-leave.

McNair, K. (1979) 'Capturing inflight decisions: thoughts while teaching'. *Educational Research Quarterly*, 3: 26–42.

Mashburn, A. J. and Pianta, R.C. (2006) 'Social relationships and school readiness'. *Early Education and Development*, 17(1): 151–176.

Maulana, R., Helms-Lorenz, M. and van de Grift, W. (2015) 'Development and evaluation of a questionnaire measuring pre-service teachers' teaching behaviour: a Rasch modelling approach'. *School Effectiveness and School Improvement*, 26: 169–194.

Merriam-Webster's Ninth New Collegiate Dictionary (1983) Springfield, MA: Merriam-Webster.

Minke, K. M., Sheridan, S. M., Kim, E. M., Ryoo, J. H. and Koziol, N. A. (2014) 'Congruence in parent–teacher relationships: the role of shared perceptions'. *Elementary School Journal*, 114(4): 527–546.

Mischel, W., Shoda, Y. and Rodriguez, M. I. (1989) 'Delay of gratification in children'. *Science*, 26(244): 933–938.

Mitchell, D. (2014) *What Really Works in Special and Inclusive Education.* Abingdon and New York: Routledge.

Montague, S. [presenter] (2014) *The Educators: John Hattie* [audio]. BBC Radio 4 (25 August). Available at: https://www.bbc.co.uk/programmes/b04dmxwl.

National Foundation for Educational Research (NFER) (2018) 'Self and peer assessment: brushing up on assessment'. Available at: https://www.nfer.ac.uk/media/3113/self_and_peer_assessment.pdf.

National PTA (2000) *Building Successful Partnerships: A Guide for Developing Parent and Family Involvement Programs*. Bloomington, IN: National PTA/National Education Service.

Newcomer, L. L. and Lewis, T. J. (2004) 'Functional behavioral assessment: an investigation of assessment reliability and effectiveness of function-based interventions'. *Journal of Emotional and Behavioral Disorders*, 12: 168–181.

Newman, F. M. and Wehlage, G. G. (1997) *Successful School Restructuring: A Report to the Public and Educators*. Available at: https://files.eric.ed.gov/fulltext/ED387925.pdf.

Nussbaumer, A., Dahrendorf, D., Schmitz, H. C., Kravcik, M., Berthold, M. and Albert, D. (2014) 'Recommender and guidance strategies for creating personal mashup learning environments'. *Computer Science and Information Systems*, 11: 321–342.

Ofsted (2019) *Inspecting the Curriculum* (May). Available at: https://www.gov.uk/government/publications/inspecting-the-curriculum.

Onwuegbuzie, A. J. and Frels, R. (2016) *Seven Steps to a Comprehensive Literature Review: A Multimodal and Cultural Approach*. London: SAGE.

Organisation for Economic Co-operation and Development (OECD) (2015) *Equity and Quality in Education: Supporting Disadvantaged Students and Schools*. Paris: OECD. Available at: http://www.oecd.org/education/school/equityandqualityineducation-supportingdisadvantagedstudentsandschools.htm.

Pajares, M. F. (1992) 'Teachers' beliefs and educational research: cleaning up a messy construct'. *Review of Educational Research*, 62(3): 307–332.

Pashler, H., McDaniel, M., Rohrer, D. and Bjork, R. (2008) 'Learning styles: concepts and evidence'. *Psychological Science in the Public Interest*, 9(3): 105–119.

Patton, G., Bond, L., Butler, H. and Glover, S. (2003) 'Changing schools, changing health? Design and implementation of the Gatehouse Project'. *Journal of Adolescent Health*, 33: 231–239.

Pavlik Jr, P. I., and Anderson, J. R. (2005) 'Practice and forgetting effects on vocabulary memory: an activation based model of the spacing effect'. *Cognitive Science*, 29: 559–586.

Pinkett, M. and Roberts, M. (2019) *Boys Don't Try? Rethinking Masculinity in Schools*. Abingdon and New York: Routledge.

Pintrich, P. R. and Zusho, A. (2001) 'Goal orientation and self-regulated learning in the college classroom: a cross-cultural comparison'. In F. Salili and C. Chiu (eds), *Student Motivation: The Culture and Context of Learning*. Dordrecht: Kluwer Academic Publishers, pp. 149–169.

Pyc, M. A. and Rawson, K. A. (2009) 'Testing the retrieval effort hypothesis: does greater difficulty correctly recalling information lead to higher levels of memory?' *Journal of Memory and Language*, 60: 437–447.

Quigley, A. (2012) 'Questioning – top ten strategies'. *The Confident Teacher* (10 November). Available at: https://www.theconfidentteacher.com/2012/11/questioning-top-ten-strategies.

Rana, J. and Burgin, S. (2017) 'Teaching and learning tips 2: cognitive load theory'. *International Journal of Dermatology*, 56(12): 1438–1441.

Rawson, K. A. and Van Overschelde, J. P. (2008) 'How does knowledge promote memory? The distinctiveness theory of skilled memory'. *Journal of Memory and Language*, 58: 646–668.

Reif, F. (2008) *Applying Cognitive Science to Education: Thinking and Learning in Scientific and Other Complex Domains*. Cambridge, MA: MIT Press.

Renkl, A. (2005) 'The worked example principle in multimedia learning'. In R. E. Mayer (ed.), *The Cambridge Handbook of Multimedia Learning*. Cambridge: Cambridge University Press, pp. 229–246.

Renkl, A. and Atkinson, R. K. (2007) 'An example order for cognitive skill acquisition'. In F. E. Ritter, J. Nerb, E. Lehtinen and T. M, O'Shea (eds), *In Order to Learn: How the Sequence of Topics Influence Learning*. New York: Oxford University Press, pp. 95–105.

Rich, P. R., Van Loon, M. H., Dunlosky, J. and Zaragoza, M. S. (2017) 'Belief in corrective feedback for common misconceptions: implications for knowledge revision'. *Journal of Experimental Psychology. Learning, Memory and Cognition*, 43(3): 492–501.

Robinson, W. (2014) *A Learning Profession? Teachers and Their Professional Development in England and Wales 1920–2000*. Rotterdam: Sense Publishers.

Roediger III, H. L. and Karpicke, J. D. (2006) 'The power of testing memory: basic research and implications for educational practice'. *Perspectives on Psychological Science*, 1: 181–210.

Rosenshine, B. (2012) 'Principles of instruction: research based strategies that all teachers should know'. *American Educator*, 36(1) (spring): 12–19, 39. Available at: https://www.aft.org/sites/default/files/periodicals/Rosenshine.pdf.

Rushton, I. (2011) 'How shall we know them? Trainee teachers' perceptions of their learners' abilities'. *Teaching in Lifelong Learning*, 3(1): 16–28.

Sadler, P. M., Sonnert, G., Coyle, H. P., Cook-Smith, N. and Miller, J. L. (2013) 'The influence of teachers' knowledge on student learning in middle school physical science classrooms'. *American Educational Research Journal*, 50(5): 1020–1049.

Sadler, R. (1989) 'Formative assessment and the design of instructional systems'. *Instructional Science*, 18: 119–144.

Saxe, G., Gearhart, M. and Nasir, N. S. (2001) 'Enhancing students' understanding of mathematics: a study of three contrasting approaches to professional support'. *Journal of Mathematics Teacher Education*, 4: 55–79.

Schön, D. (1983) *The Reflective Practitioner*. New York: Basic Books.

Schön, D. (1986) 'Reflection in action'. In T. J. Sergiovanni and J. E. Corbally (eds), *Leadership and Organizational Culture: New Perspectives on Administrative Theory and Practice*. Champaign, IL: University of Illinois Press, pp. 36–63.

School Home Support (2015) *Parental Engagement*. Available at: https://www.schoolhomesupport.org.uk/wp-content/uploads/2015/11/SHS-Parental-engagement-toolkit.pdf.

Sherrington, T. (2017a) *The Learning Rainforest: Great Teaching in Real Classrooms*. Woodbridge: John Catt Educational.

Sherrington, T. (2017b) 'Teaching to the top: attitudes and strategies for delivering real challenge'. *Teacherhead* (28 May). Available at: https://teacherhead.com/2017/05/28/teaching-to-the-top-attitudes-and-strategies-for-delivering-real-challenge.

Sherrington, T. (2018) 'The @teacherhead planning tool. Draft'. *Teacherhead* (30 December). Available at: https://teacherhead.com/2018/12/30/the-teacherhead-planning-tool-draft.

Sherrington, T. (2019) *Rosenshine's Principles in Action*. Woodbridge: John Catt Educational.

Shibli, D. and West, R. (2018) 'Cognitive load theory and its application in the classroom'. *Impact* (February). Available at: https://impact.chartered.college/article/shibli-cognitive-load-theory-classroom.

Singer, M. and Alexander, P. A. (2017) 'Reading on paper and digitally: what the past decades of empirical research reveal'. *Review of Educational Research*, 87(6): 1007–1041.

Sisk, V. F., Burgoyne, A. P., Sun, J., Butler, J. L. and Macnamara, B. N. (2018) 'To what extent and under which circumstances are growth mind-sets important to academic achievement? Two meta-analyses'. *Psychological Science*, 29(4): 549–571.

Steenbergen-Hu, S., Makel, C. and Olszewski-Kubilius, P. (2016) 'About the effects of ability grouping and acceleration on K-12 students' academic achievement: findings of two second-order meta-analyses'. *Review of Educational Research*, 86(4): 849–899.

Sternberg, R. (1990) *Metaphors of Mind: Conceptions of the Nature of Intelligence*. Cambridge: Cambridge University Press.

Sugai, G., Horner, R. H. and Gresham, F. M. (2002) 'Behaviorally effective school environments'. In M. R. Shinn, H. M. Walker and G. Stoner (eds), *Interventions for Academic and Behaviour Problems: Preventative and Remedial Approaches*. Bethesda, MD: National Association of School Psychologists, pp. 84–101.

Sweller, J. (2005) 'Implications of cognitive load theory for multimedia learning'. In R. E. Mayer (ed.), *The Cambridge Handbook of Multimedia Learning*. Cambridge: Cambridge University Press, pp. 19–30.

Sweller, J. (2010) 'Cognitive load theory: recent theoretical advances'. In J. Plass, R. Moreno and R. Brunken (eds), *Cognitive Load Theory*. New York: Cambridge University Press, pp. 29–47.

Sweller, J., Ayres, P. and Kalyuga, S. (2011) *Cognitive Load Theory: Explorations in the Learning Sciences, Instructional Systems and Performance Technologies*. New York: Springer.

Sweller, J., van Merrienboer, J. and Paas, F. (1998) 'Cognitive architecture and instructional design'. *Educational Psychology Review*, 10(3): 251–296.

Tarr, R. (2015) 'Takeaway homework'. *Class Tools* (12 February). Available at: www.classtools.net/blog/takeaway-homework.

Tay, C. (2018) 'A good start: the pedagogical challenge of engaging prior knowledge for all pupils'. *Impact* (May). Available at: https://impact.chartered.college/article/tay-pedagogical-challenge-engaging-prior-knowledge.

Taylor, V. J. and Walton, G. M. (2011) 'Stereotype threat undermines academic learning'. *Personality and Social Psychology Bulletin*, 37(8): 1055–1067.

Tereshchenko, A., Francis, B., Archer, L., Hodgen, J., Mazenod, A., Taylor, B., Pepper, D. and Travers, M-C. (2019) 'Learners' attitudes to mixed attainment grouping: examining the views of students of high, middle and low attainment'. *Research Papers in Education*, 34(4): 425–444.

Timperley, H. (2008) *Teacher Professional Learning and Development*. Educational Practices Series 18. Available at: http://www.ibe.unesco.org/fileadmin/user_upload/Publications/Educational_Practices/Ed Practices_18.pdf.

Tomlinson, C. A., Brighton, C., Hertberg, H., Callahan, C. M., Moon, T. R., Brimijoin, K. and Reynolds, T. (2003) 'Differentiating instruction in response to student readiness, interest and learning profile in academically diverse classrooms: a review of literature'. *Journal for the Education of the Gifted*, 27: 119–145.

Torff, B. (1999) 'Tacit knowledge in teaching: folk pedagogy and teacher education'. In R. Sternberg and J. Horvath (eds), *Tacit Knowledge in Professional Practice: Researcher and Practitioner Perspectives*. Mahwah, NJ: Lawrence Erlbaum, pp. 44–65.

Truss, E. (2013) 'Elizabeth Truss speaks to education publishers about curriculum reform' [speech] (2 December). Available at: https://www.gov.uk/government/speeches/elizabeth-truss-speaks-to-education-publishers-about-curriculum-reform.

University College London (2019) *UCL Verbal Feedback Project Report 2019*. Available at: https://www.ucl.ac.uk/widening-participation/sites/widening-participation/files/2019_verbal_feedback_project_final_4_print.pdf.

Ursache, A., Blair, C. and Raver, C. C. (2012) 'The promotion of self-regulation as a means of enhancing school readiness and early achievement in children at risk for school failure'. *Child Development Perspectives*, 6(2): 122–128.

Valiente, C., Lemery-Chalfant, K., Swanson, J. and Reiser, M. (2008) 'Prediction of children's academic competence from their effortful control, relationships, and classroom participation'. *Journal of Educational Psychology*, 100: 67–77.

van de Grift, W. (2007) 'Quality of teaching in four European countries: a review of the literature and application of an assessment instrument'. *Educational Research*, 49: 127–152.

van de Grift, W., van der Wal, M. and Torenbeek, M. (2011) 'Ontwikkeling in de pedagogische didactische vaardigheid van leraren in het basisonderwijs' [Development of the pedagogical didactical competences of teachers in primary education]. *Pedagogische Studiën*, 88: 416–432.

Van Gog, T., Paas, F. and van Merrienboer, J. J. (2004) 'Process-orientated worked example: improving transfer performance through enhanced understanding. *Instructional Science*, 32: 83–98.

Vygotsky, L. S. (1978) *Mind in Society: The Development of Higher Psychological Processes*. Cambridge, MA: Harvard University Press.

Waterford (2018) 'How parent involvement leads to student success' (1 November). Available at: https://www.waterford.org/education/how-parent-involvment-leads-to-student-success.

Weale, S. (2019) 'Fifth of teachers plan to leave profession within two years'. *The Guardian* (16 April). Available at: https://www.theguardian.com/education/2019/apr/16/fifth-of-teachers-plan-to-leave-profession-within-two-years.

Webb, J. (2019) *How to Teach English Literature: Overcoming Cultural Poverty*. Woodbridge: John Catt Educational.

Wei, R. C., Darling-Hammond, L., Andree, A., Richardson, N. and Orphanos, S. (2009) *Professional Learning in the Learning Profession: A Status Report on Teacher Development in the United States and Abroad*. Available at: https://edpolicy.stanford.edu/sites/default/files/publications/professional-learning-learning-profession-status-report-teacher-development-us-and-abroad.pdf.

Weinstein, R. S. (2002) *Reaching Higher: The Power of Expectations in Schooling*. Cambridge, MA: Harvard University Press.

Werner, E. E. and Smith, R. S. (1992) *Overcoming the Odds: High-Risk Children from Birth to Adulthood*. Ithaca, NY: Cornell University Press.

Wertsch, J. V. (1979) 'From social interaction to higher psychological process: a clarification of Vygotsky's theory'. *Human Development*, 22: 1–22.

Wiliam, D. (2011) *Embedded Formative Assessment*. Bloomington, IN: Solution Tree Press.

Wiliam, D. (2017a) Assessment, marking and feedback. In C. Hendrick and R. Macpherson (eds), *What Does This Look Like in the Classroom? Bridging the Gap Between Research and Practice*. Woodbridge: John Catt Educational, pp. 29–57.

Wiliam, D. (2017b) 'I've come to the conclusion Sweller's Cognitive Load Theory is the single most important thing for teachers to know' [tweet] (26 January). Available at: https://twitter.com/dylanwiliam/status/824682504602943489?lang=en.

Wiliam, D. and Leahy, S. (2015) *Embedding Formative Assessment: Practical Techniques for K-12 Classrooms*. West Palm Beach, FL: Learning Sciences International.

Wiliam, D. and Leahy, S. (2017) *Sustaining Formative Assessment with Teacher Learning Communities*. Available at: https://www.dylanwiliamcenter.com/sfa-with-tlcs.

Wiliam, D., Leahy, S., Lyon, C. and Thompson, M. (2005) 'Classroom assessment: minute by minute, day by day'. *Educational Leadership*, 63(3): 19–24.

Wiliam, D. and Thompson, M. (2007) 'Integrating assessment with learning: what will it take to make it work?' In C. A. Dwyer (ed.), *The Future of Assessment: Shaping Teaching and Learning*. Mahwah, NJ: Lawrence Erlbaum, pp. 53–82.

Williams, J. (2018) *It Just Grinds You Down: Persistent Disruptive Behaviour in Schools and What Can Be Done About It*. Available at: https://policyexchange.org.uk/wp-content/uploads/2019/01/It-Just-Grinds-You-Down-Joanna-Williams-Policy-Exchange-December-2018.pdf.

Willingham, D. T. (2009) *Why Don't Students Like School? A Cognitive Scientist Answers Questions About How the Mind Works and What It Means for the Classroom*. San Francisco, CA: Jossey-Bass.

Willingham, D. T. (2010) 'The myth of learning styles'. *Change*, 42(5): 32–35.

Willoughby, T. and Wood, E. (1994) 'Elaborative interrogation examined at encoding and retrieval'. *Learning and Instruction*, 4: 139–149.

Wittwer, J. and Renkl, A. (2010) 'How effective are instructional explanations in example-based learning? A meta-analytic review'. *Educational Psychology Review*, 22(4): 393–409.

Wolf, G. (1996) 'Steve Jobs: the next insanely great thing'. *Wired* (1 February). Available at: https://www.wired.com/1996/02/jobs-2.

Wood, D., Bruner, J. S. and Ross, G. (1976) 'The role of tutoring in problem solving'. *Journal of Child Psychology and Psychiatry and Allied Disciplines*, 17: 89–100.

Zimmerman, B. J. (2000) 'Self-efficacy: an essential motive to learn'. *Contemporary Educational Psychology*, 25(1): 82–91.

Zimmerman, B. J. (2002) 'Becoming a self-regulated learner: an overview'. *Theory Into Practice*, 41(2): 64–70.

About the author

Haili Hughes is an English teacher and a former head of department and senior leader who has mentored new teachers and ITT students for over ten years.

From her working class roots of growing up on a council estate in the north-west of England, she worked several jobs to put herself through college and university and earn her degree in English. She went on to win a prestigious graduate trainee position at the *News of the World* newspaper in London, where she worked on their news and features desks before deciding to retrain as a teacher and do something a bit more morally satisfying.

She has now been teaching for the best part of 15 years and has enjoyed developing and supporting teachers at many different stages of their career – from student teacher to head of department. She is also passionate about keeping experienced staff in the classroom and helping to retain experienced teachers who may feel like they are somewhat jaded with the profession. Her role in school is to work with the most able learners, particularly those from disadvantaged backgrounds, to raise aspirations and to train staff to ensure that they are challenging pupils and developing their pedagogy to meet their needs.

In her spare time, she writes regular articles for the *TES* and other education publications, and also peer reviews submissions for the Chartered College of Teaching's *Impact* journal. She recently completed her third master's degree in psychology and is currently in her third year of her doctorate at the University of Glasgow. She lives in the countryside, surrounded by moors, lakes and stunning landscapes with her husband Mike and two children Hendrix and Frida.

The Five-Minute Coach

Improve Performance – Rapidly

ISBN: 978-184590800-3

Lynne Cooper and Mariette Castellino

Designed for leaders, managers and supervisors in any setting, *The Five-Minute Coach* is a groundbreaking approach to coaching on the job. It creates significant performance improvements, whilst improving job satisfaction for manager and team member alike. This approach to coaching has been developed by the authors and used in organisations across the board large and small, private and public, with adults and teens, and across a variety of voluntary and community groups. Professional coaches have also adopted The Five-Minute Coach in their work.

The book leads the reader through this deceptively simple process which changes thinking about how to work with others. Leaders no longer need to have all the answers. They benefit from true delegation. They uncover the talent and resources of others. They free up time for themselves – time to think strategically and to be more proactive, creative and innovative.

With its focus on outcome-thinking, effective action planning and motivating people to take action, the book offers clear steps, practical examples and tips. It all adds up to a very practical way to improve performance.